NEVER GO BROKE

Lee Boyce & Jesse McClure

NEVER
GO
BROKE

How to make money out of just about anything

First published in Great Britain in 2021 by Cassell, an imprint of
Octopus Publishing Group Ltd
Carmelite House
50 Victoria Embankment
London EC4Y 0DZ
www.octopusbooks.co.uk

An Hachette UK Company
www.hachette.co.uk

ISBN 978-1-78840-295-8

A CIP catalogue record for this book is available from the British Library.

Printed and bound in Great Britain

10 9 8 7 6 5 4 3 2 1

This FSC® label means that materials used for the product
have been responsibly sourced

Publishing Director: Stephanie Jackson
Senior Editor: Pauline Bache
Copy Editor: Joanne Smith
Art Director: Jaz Bahra
Typesetter: Jeremy Tilston at The Oak Studio
Cover Designer: Jonathan Christie
Senior Production Controller: Emily Noto

JM: I love you, Nicole.

LB: For Brooke and Danielle.

THIS BOOK WILL MAKE YOU MONEY

STEP 1. BUILD UP A FREE CASH POT

STEP 2. LEARN YOUR RESALE BLUEPRINT

STEP 3. INVEST THE POT FOR EASY RESALE PROFITS

CONTENTS

PART III: PRACTICAL PLACES TO BAG PROFITS

FOREWORD

SURVIVING OR EVEN THRIVING DURING ECONOMIC TURMOIL

In 2020, a pandemic swept the globe and hit many countries hard. As we write this, both the UK and the US face a huge wave of job losses – far greater than the financial crash of 2007/8. We are entering the unknown. Never before have so many nations felt the need to hit the big red pause button simultaneously: it is a scary new world, with financial worries and strife on the agenda for millions of people.

The internet will be full of worried, flapping fish who have never faced hardship like this before, never in their wildest nightmares thought it could happen to them. Many have had to sign up for benefits perhaps for the first time, investors – both experienced and novice – are riding stock-market storms and many people have had to tap into their savings (if they were lucky enough to have some). It is likely economic turmoil is going to exist for some time to come, including record low, or even negative, interest rates. The virus has unleashed a vicious and brutal tsunami of financial pain for all classes of people.

However, despite this gloom, we're here to tell you that everything is going to be okay. If you follow the tips in this book, we can help you survive economic upheaval and even thrive once the dust settles, by honing your resale skills and tapping simple opportunities. A fish back in water.

That's why we have written a foreword specifically for these tough economic times we're living in – it wasn't planned in the original draft of the book.

Spotting pandemic trends, today AND in the future

Recently we've been inundated with questions about personal finance. Some of those questions have included: just how am I going to survive this crash? What can I do to get myself out of a hole? Should I just sell all my possessions to make ends meet?

These questions come from those who have lost their jobs, careers and hope. They are themed around every aspect of everyday finance, from mortgages to savings, pensions to car ownership, grocery shopping to worries about how their families are going to get by.

We've also been inundated with questions about specific possessions: how much is this comic book I've held in pristine condition in my top drawer worth now? Should I just sell my car? What items can I look out for around the home that can net me some short-term funds? You can't eat comic books, cars or domestic items, but you can sell them for cold, hard cash to swap for food, or to make ends meet.

We can help you with the perfect financial formula to answer all these questions. Lee has the skills to read and understand the data and news as it comes in. Jesse can turn that into a real-life strategy to fit your own personal circumstances. For example, it was recently reported that ski resorts around Europe are closing. So what? Why do we care? Firstly, if this trend continues, it is likely it will affect your local resort. If that is the case, we can assume the short-term demand for ski boots, snowboards and winter paraphernalia will decrease dramatically.

What do we do then? Buy low? Sell as quickly as possible? That's the point of *Never Go Broke*. We'll help you spot trends and demand hot spots and make money from them.

We will explain why you shouldn't panic-sell, how you potentially have a huge untapped household wealth you're not even aware of and show you ways to ensure you never go broke. Use the advice in this book to apply to the current situation as it unfolds.

How to survive

Surviving this financial impact will mean you in brace position on an aircraft heading down. But there are ways to survive. We'll show you how to value the contents of your home and tot up a net worth you didn't even realize you had.

Let's not kid ourselves – everyone has different items in their homes, which vary in quantity, quality and value so it's pointless for us to explain how to sell a specific item. But resale can be likened to a 'magic formula', which we'll explore throughout the lessons in this book. We can offer you a general framework on which to base your decisions when it comes to buying and selling literally anything.

So, dear readers, we'll give you all the information you need to sell your Blu-ray copy of *Happy Feet*. 'Lee, Jesse…I don't own this terrible movie, nor do I own a Blu-ray player! What gives?'

The movie title and format don't matter. What matters is finding an outlet that buys all media types. If you have books rather than CDs, PlayStation games rather than DVDs, the means to find that maximum value will nearly always be the same.

We will guide you, whatever you're trying to sell – however weird, wonderful or common it may be. And we won't judge you for your taste in penguin-themed flicks.

How to thrive

Thriving means you stepping into the cockpit and steering the plane up again, by mastering the secrets of buying and selling. First, we'll teach you how to build a pot of no-risk, free cash. From there, we'll help you establish a resale blueprint, before taking a tour of the places you can reinvest that money for profits.

You'll be inspired and soon realize how good you can get at this. You might even end up with a full-time career in buying and selling, or a side-hustle business where you can turn enough profit to never go broke – recession or no recession.

The pandemic panicked people into trying to offload items quickly and that is likely to exacerbate in the coming years. That means there will be opportunities to pick up unloved items on the cheap, to flip for a tidy profit – if you know what you're looking for, take your time and know where to sell them, using resources available to everyone.

How to create wealth for a buy-in

As the pandemic unfolded, Jesse began to prepare for what could be a huge buying-in opportunity. Simply put, there were going to be items – the contents of people's homes and more – that would be sold far too cheaply and Jesse would be around to sniff them out and flip them for a profit. That, in a nutshell, is his job as a Resale King. You shouldn't view it as taking advantage, more being prepared.

In order to do this, he started saving up money before the pandemic fully took hold, adding to a pot he had already built for a buying opportunity like this (although he never imagined one quite like this). He sold off items that became hot to create a liquid fund to take advantage of the buying opportunities ahead.

For example, one of the hottest lockdown items was the Nintendo Switch console. He had bought his, along with some games, for around $400 in autumn 2019. Seeing that the pandemic had created the need for a silly escape from reality, Jesse sold his console – well used – on a local online selling website for nearly double what he'd paid for it.

It was an issue of supply and demand: Nintendo were struggling to fill the retailers' shelves quickly enough as people lined up for the must-have console to help pass the pandemic time at home. At the other end of this scale are the items people were trying to shift at rock-bottom prices – consumers were nervier about spending their cash and many weren't spending at all.

Throughout the book, we will highlight just how you can take advantage and spot the buying and selling opportunities open to you.

We all have a household net worth

To help create a pot of money to invest in resale, there has never been a better opportunity to walk around your home and note down your total net worth – of you as an individual or as a family. Many say they are poor or struggling to make ends meet, failing to realize the thousands of pounds they are likely to have lurking around the home. And a large chunk of this worth is often in items you no longer use or care about. CDs, DVDs, books, video games, clothes, gadgets, jewellery, metals, toys and even your rubbish can be sold on for varying levels of profit.

The first part of the book is crammed with information on how to get the right price for your stuff, and create an income jar so you are ready to pounce at any opportunity.

It is worth pointing out that many people simply think 'boring' items have no value – that they should be thrown away. Are you guilty of throwing perfectly good clothes into those metal donation containers? Do you visit the local tip to ditch goods you've tired of? Have you hired a skip to chuck away your 'junk'?

If the answer is yes to any of these questions, it's time to rethink and repeat the mantra: *everything has value*. This is especially true now in a time of economic crisis and environmental concern.

Other ways to save money

Although *Never Go Broke* is mostly about buying and selling, Lee has
a background in personal finance and shares some easy ways to save
money and make sure you are not making common money mistakes
that could be rectified in minutes.

For example, how many of us are guilty of over consuming? Of not
saving money properly or relying on credit? Of not looking around for
simple voucher codes? Dotted throughout the lessons are quick and
easy wins to help ensure you never go broke.

Economic crisis creates opportunity

We've seen many economic crises throughout the history of
humankind – from self-inflicted bubbles to contagious economic panic
created by global banks. In these events, there are always winners and
losers. We're not here to make sure you're a winner but we will guide
you through ways to avoid going broke and to tap the opportunities
that are out there. Much of your success will depend on how much
effort you put in.

Find the panic, don't be part of it. More than likely, an opportunity
will arise.

Panic leads to mistakes

Under all circumstances, panicked people make costly mistakes and
a pandemic is no different. This pandemic earthquake will cause
aftershocks that will see opportunity arise as people rush to sell items
cheaply, not taking the time to have them valued properly. It is all about
looking to seize the opportunity and having the right tools to do so.

When it comes to buying and selling, goods are only worth what
someone is willing to pay, whether that is property or coins, cars or
comic books. With the expert knowledge you'll glean from this book,

you'll know how to sell and buy correctly, to strike at the right time, exploiting niches and going through the right channels.

JESSE'S DREAM CAR...A FERRARI OR A PRIUS?

During the last financial crisis, prices for vintage Ferraris slumped. These beautiful beasts – despite their glory – have heavy maintenance costs, high insurance premiums and fuel costs. In a financial crisis, all expensive classic cars become bloated, greedy elephants on the driveway or in storage.

I was willing to take on that burden, and managed to find a pristine 1981 red Ferrari 308 for the amazing price of $28,000. A Ferrari for under $30,000? Yes please! I arranged an appointment and drove to a gentleman's house to check out this stallion.

As I approached the five-car garage, a clearly out of place but nearly new Prius blocked the way to my new luxury ride. The seller apologized for the inconvenience. I saw a potential opportunity. I asked, 'How much for the Prius?'.

'You can have it for $1,000.'

'Excuse me?'

'Yeah, I bought this goofy thing brand new for my daughter, but she doesn't like it. I just want this weird thing off my driveway...'

I didn't even look at the Ferrari. For $1,000, I ended up with a car I've driven for 14 years and 250,000 miles, with superb fuel efficiency – and only with the small proviso of looking a bit 'goofy'.

That little Prius is the best car I've ever owned. Always expect the unexpected and ask questions about other items, as we'll explain further.

Sometimes, a Prius is a better option than a Ferrari. Really.

Adapting to lockdown and the aftermath

One of the biggest adjustments we in the Western world have ever had to make, at least in recent decades, was adapting to lockdown. But the world of buying, selling and money continued. One huge difference between lockdown 2020 as opposed to, say, a lockdown 20 years ago, is the internet. The internet makes the entire world your marketplace.

Whether it's selling a used pram on a local website to someone in your neighbourhood, or a rare stamp to a collector in the nether regions of New Zealand, lockdown didn't stop that. Post Offices were open, the postal service still in operation and deliveries were frequently arriving on people's doorsteps from a wide range of different companies – big and small – albeit with occasional delays.

But the point is this: the world of trading didn't simply stop. The internet kept things going and it can be your best friend when it comes to selling items. We'll teach you to find the right market for your specific items.

Marketplaces have been hit

In some ways, you could argue that lockdown helped create a stronger demand and faith in buying items online. The majority of people working from home for the first time relied on these services to get by – whether it was food delivered to their doors, medicine or a paddling pool to keep the kids occupied.

It also created the time for people to go through their old items to list and sell online – maybe a wardrobe clear-out or the chance to get in the loft and look through those old boxes. There were no excuses for not using the time to advertise items. What else was there to do?

That being said, some of the selling events we mention in the book were temporarily suspended or scaled down thanks to social distancing (boot sales and auctions, for example). But despite this, when they have been allowed to reopen, they have come back bigger and stronger than ever. Britons love a boot sale. Americans love a yard sale.

Since the dawn of time, humans have enjoyed physical interaction while buying and selling goods – through wars, plagues and outside Madonna gigs. This won't stop – things will get back to normal, even if that normal includes social distancing, hand sanitizer and face masks.

At first buyers might be hesitant to get back out in a large crowd. But sellers will still be desperate to sell their items as quick as before (and probably cheaper). Don't risk your health, of course, but be aware of this upcoming opportunity.

Never done it before? No problem!

If there are any positives to take from resale during a pandemic, it's the following:

- You'll realize there are ways to never go broke – these are simple tips and tricks that can be learned easily.
- There are going to be opportunities to make some tidy profits.
- It is likely you are sitting on a little personal goldmine of consumables worth £1,000–£20,000, which can be used to buy and sell, and make money.
- You should never be embarrassed to haggle. If people can bulk buy toilet paper and not feel ashamed, there is nothing to fear when it comes to getting stuck in.

By the time you've finished this book, we guarantee you'll be inspired to become an occasional resale player, a part-time one or even a fully fledged mini Jesse. Boys and girls, things may get tougher out there, but sooner or later we will get back to a (somewhat) normal way of life. Take advantage of this downtime as an opportunity, not a burden.

Right, enough of this pandemic chat – let's get stuck in!

NEVER GO BROKE IN A NUTSHELL

This book will make you money. Let's skip the feel-good quotes and hype and get down to it.

We've read dozens of business, self-help, personal finance and investing books. *Never Go Broke* is different. It's not a teaching tool, revealing all the secrets of becoming the world's greatest salesperson. Don't get us wrong, we will show you direct links and information on ways to buy and sell. But the key thing we will teach you is to use easily available and existing resources to your advantage.

Making money is fun and can be easy, if you know where to look and how to apply yourself.

There are no prerequisites to success in using this book. You do not need a special degree in quantum finance physics or years of experience in the world of antiques. This is for absolutely anyone who wants to better themselves financially, using their brain and some hard work to achieve the simple goal of more money in their pocket. Is that you?

There is no cap on how much money you can make. How far you want to take it is up to you. If you are looking to make a couple of extra quid, then this book has more than enough information for you to achieve that. If you are on the brink of financial collapse or have had a seismic shock to your personal finances, you could potentially use *Never Go Broke* to help turn your financial prospects around immediately.

We will help you discover the value in yourself and any items you find, helping you become your own appraiser and teaching you how to find the answers yourself. This book is made for people who want to help themselves.

Do you want to know the secret of never going broke? How you can make tidy profits buying and selling? Why you should take stock of every item in your home and find out how everything – yes, everything – has value? You've come to the right place.

Here we unleash unique tricks, tips, insights and anecdotes on how to make easy cash with minimal effort. Drawing on our unheralded experience and expertise, we'll reveal the golden basics to never going broke, the practical ways to make money and the secrets to buying and selling success in three easy-to-digest parts.

We'll be giving out tips for all levels, taking you from resale novice, through intermediate and finally to pro, by the time you've finished.

We'll help you build a free pot of cash from ground zero, teaching you tricks to establish your own personal resale blueprint before you dive in and take that little mound of wealth you've created and invest it in the practical places to flip easy profits.

Are you ready to become a Resale King or Queen? Of course you are…

ABOUT US

Hi. I'm Jesse McClure. You may remember me from television shows such as *Storage Hunters* and *British Treasure, American Gold*. They pulled in millions of viewers and I am immensely proud of them. In order to get my break on *Storage Hunters*, I played the antagonist. I was to the television show what John McEnroe was to the tennis world – a handsome rogue people loved to hate, with epic sideburns and tantrums to boot.

But, being honest, that isn't what I'm really about. It's what I had to do to make a name for myself and I'm glad I did – it helped make Brand Jesse. I also learned many great lessons and met fascinating (and some irritating) buyers and sellers along the way.

I often think of *Storage Hunters* as my biggest ever sell. I sold myself, got onto the show and my life has never been the same since.

I chose the antagonist persona on the programme not because I have an aggressive, negative energy, but because I had to do something different to stand out. It can be an act I use while bargain hunting, depending on the circumstances. I found a money-making opportunity in the form of *Storage Hunters* and I took advantage of it. It was the best investment I've ever made.

What you may not realize is that I do have serious credentials when it comes to buying and selling. I genuinely believe I am a Resale King (if not *the* Resale King) and over the course of this book, you'll see why. I'll be revealing all of my secrets, tips and tricks to help you make some serious dosh. You really can make money for old rope – well, you say 'old', I say 'vintage'. It's easier than you think.

Am I the best seller in the world? Don't tell my ego, but probably not. But what I'll teach you will give you the confidence to become a Resale King or Queen too…and no one will be able to tell you otherwise.

Buying and selling to turn tasty profits is in my blood – I'm like a money-making vampire: cut me and I bleed green. Since I stepped out of nappies I have been learning the trade. I've sold everything, from pennies to Porsches. You name it, the likelihood is I've flogged it at some time, or at least have some knowledge of it.

My parents run one of the oldest antiques shops in Los Angeles and I have seen thousands of weird and wonderful items pass through, from dead animals and bones to weird medical equipment. For example, in recent years, I sold Western-style items to a buyer who eventually turned around and told me she was gathering them for a Harrison Ford flick. When I watched the movie, I spotted dozens of items I had sourced and sold to her from the shop. It's a fun and varied living.

By the time I was 12 years old, I'd acquired more than a hundred gaming arcade machines from nothing, just by trading and haggling – I'll tell you more in a later lesson. I'd caught the bug. Now in my 30s and having had many successes (mixed with a few failures) in my buying and selling career, I feel it is time to share my secrets with you.

But I'm not doing it alone. Award-winning financial journalist, writer and fellow bargain-hunter Lee Boyce has delved into my brain to reveal all you need to know to make money from pretty much nothing. And he has his own tips as well. You have bought this book. You can read it, make some money and then sell it again (if you want). Or you may want to keep it on your bookshelf for all eternity to help you make money when you need it. It's your call.

Lee was Consumer Affairs Editor at the world's biggest newspaper website – the Mail Online – for many years before being promoted to Assistant Editor of the hugely popular money section, *This is Money*. At the weekends, Lee regularly visits car boot sales and antiques markets searching for a bargain to sell on. He does it more as a hobby, whereas for me it's a profession.

Over the last decade, Lee has helped millions of people save money and battle financial giants who have treated readers unfairly. David versus Goliath stuff. He was the natural fit to help me write this book.

I had come across Lee's name frequently while researching bank notes and coins online as I sniffed out information like a Labrador. We bonded over pretzels and Twiglets while talking about our mutual interest in coins and bank notes. Lee is a large reason Britons have gone coin- and note-collecting crazy. He wrote a story about the rare coins that can turn up in your change and it was read by millions of people.

We realized we have a lot in common, including our youth and attitudes to thriftiness. When I was younger, my father would save up grocery vouchers each week to obtain some serious discounts at the store. One time he paid just a couple of bucks for a $150 shop. That made me see just how much (or little) people can pay or overpay when it comes to everyday life.

When I told this tale to Lee, he smiled. He told me a story of how he and his father, when he was growing up in Essex, would do a Saturday morning 'womble'.

Wombling, he tells me, is where you hunt around the supermarket car park looking for receipts. On many receipts were unclaimed points for the supermarket loyalty card. They would scoop them up, come rain or shine, take them to customer services and load the points onto their card. Twenty minutes of work could result in a half-price shop.

We both realized the profound effect these grocery shopping experiences had in shaping our attitude to money. We were brought up well with parents in good jobs – but they never lost sight of how to avoid overspending. Being thrifty was a way of life.

I still use coupons, eat off the dollar menu and shop at thrift stores for my clothes. Why? Because it's in my DNA. I cannot resist a bargain. And Lee won't pay full price at McDonald's on the rare occasion he goes. He'll always snip out coupons from the free daily newspapers handed out in London.

See? We were destined to write this book together! We love money. Saving it. Making it. Eating it. Talking about it.

The other unique perspective I can give is how things work both in the US and the UK. I flit between the two and will usually be found in one of three places: Lancashire, London or California. The latter is a touch sunnier and warmer, but doesn't quite have the same standard of tea or accents.

Making money is increasingly a global affair – even if you're doing it from the comfort of your own home. The fundamentals are the same no matter where you are in the world – you just have little quirks in the market, which we will come on to explain.

Lastly, Lee and I both like an underdog. I support Accrington Stanley Football Club, while Lee supports Southend United. Neither of these teams will ever be world-beaters, but these smaller community clubs usually have heart, spirit and the right attitude.

These are traits you will need to become a Resale King.

We hope you enjoy reading this book as much as we have enjoyed writing it.

OUR MANTRA

The mantra that runs through the entirety of this book is this:
This is not a get-rich-quick book – it's a never-go-broke book.

Many get-rich-quick books are stuck in the past, with tacky fonts and colourful covers. They promise a step-by-step path to building huge wealth, often targeted at those who have inherited a sizable trust fund or have large sums to play with after they've paid their bills.

But whether you have lots of money, no money or are somewhere in between, it is likely you're thinking about the green stuff at least once a day. Money on the brain.

We'll arm you with the knowledge you need to make some lovely profits using everyday ideas which we've seen work many times. It is unlikely we'll make you millionaires overnight (seriously, if those get-rich-quick books worked, we'd all be like Biff Tannen in *Back to the Future II*, right?) but we can almost guarantee you won't go broke if you follow our tips – all for the price of four takeaway coffees or five Lotto tickets. Surely this is a better investment?

We believe it is easy to teach people how to buy and sell. That is why this book exists. It has been two decades times two in the making – we're offloading secrets we've learned over the years.

People within the resale game often pigeonhole themselves into niche areas, whether it's trading cars, sports cards, coins or taxidermy. But the core principle stays the same no matter what you collect: everything has value. Even stuffed pets. That's what really intrigued me about getting into the business. I focused on video games first of all – when I was younger and more naive – not because I had visions of becoming an arcade mogul, but simply because I enjoyed them.

Buying items you enjoy rather than thinking about the money-making perspective lowers your chance of failure at the beginning and enhances your excitement. That is often the best foundation to build from – make it part of a hobby with an untapped ceiling of how far you can go. It's the healthiest approach and better than trying to chase the mythical million and fall into a trap.

You may be collecting something and waiting to sell at the optimum time, or keeping it to pass down the generations. Or maybe you need to flog some wares for emergency cash. People all around the globe are doing the same thing, and always have been.

Buying and selling has been an art form since humankind began. Tribes would barter to swap goods. Even in those times, thousands of years ago, some Neanderthals probably knew how to get a far better deal than others. Who knows, maybe one of these early humans once claimed to be the Resale King. Maybe I'm related to him and my official title is Resale King Jesse XVI, ancestor of the ultimate Resale King of Arabia who traded in rugs.

Too far?

Whether goods are bartered on the Silk Road, where exotic wares were brought from the East to the West, or traded on modern-day online marketplaces, where goods sell in an instant with a click from anywhere in the world, there are tricks, tips and easy things you can do to make a crust. Whether that crust is a hobby, a side business, a way to supplement your income or eventually your only source of income, we have the sound advice you need in the coming lessons.

If you want to empty your home, perhaps inspired by Marie Kondo, don't just take your things to the tip – realize their value and resale potential. That's good for the environment as well as your wallet.

If you have conjured up images of that scene in *Wolf of Wall Street* where the protagonist starts with 'sell this pen', that is not what this book is about. If that's what you were after, you'll be sorely disappointed. Perhaps list this book for sale and see if you can make a profit on it before you dive in and waste your time. Instead, we'll be teaching you how to start from scratch and that everything, yes everything, has value.

But let us be clear here: we do not know the value and eBay selling price of every item ever created in human existence and neither will you...sorry. But we'll use our vast expertise to show you that you won't have to.

You can learn the art of buying and selling in a variety of ways, from charity shops to antique markets, the internet to car boot sales. You might want to read the whole book at once or pluck out parts of it like a magpie, storing little titbits of information that are relevant to you.

We can make you a Resale King or Queen. If you want, you can buy a crown and throne (but only if you haggle for them).

THE GOAL

Our goal is not to make you rich, although it'll be a beautiful bonus if it does. It is to make sure you never go broke. But you've got that by now, right?

We want to teach you how to become your own appraiser. You can buy and sell items yourself, you don't need me or some expert on television to guide you into making the right decision. You don't need stacks of guide books or price guides to see whether or not something is worth its price. This book will teach you to buy and sell confidently using very straightforward, strong concepts.

Part I will help you build up an exposure-free pot of cash through a number of methods, including selling unwanted items in your home, spotting freebies and spending a bit of time online.

Part II will help you build a resale blueprint, teaching you the basics. This includes recognizing that everything has value, putting a price on your time and learning the importance of building contacts.

Then we end with the fun part: where to find all of the untapped opportunities to make profits – from charity shops to boot sales, speciality auctions to antiques markets, using your free money made at the start. Our goal is to hone your resale skills.

LESSON 0: HOW TO USE THIS BOOK

We want you to use this book for inspiration, whether that is to help you survive during a period of economic uncertainty or simply to make some extra spending money to enjoy life. It may even give you the power and inspiration to go pro, like me.

The three parts of the book are broken into different lessons, each with subsections. Let's say you're not that interested in coins (for which we have a subsection). Just skip it and move on to the next subsection – or read, glean the knowledge and start flogging coins for more than their face value. It's up to you.

It's a good idea to reread a section before you attempt to sell any items you have, or if you're about to visit a charity shop or boot sale for the first time, or list goods online. The tips we've taught you will really sink in and the selling tales we offer will give you extra inspiration.

OUR PROMISE

Our promise to you is that if you follow our tips, you will make money. Both of us have decades of experience when it comes to buying, selling and recognizing the consumer pitfalls to dodge.

By the time you've finished this book, we promise to have guided you through the baby steps of making money from resale using a pot of cash you've built from nowhere.

If you read this book cover to cover you'll get bitten by the buying and selling bug. It'll burrow under your skin and give you a resale itch you may never have realized you had. You'll never want to just simply bin things ever again.

We promise that, by the end, you'll realize everything has value and you'll never look at items in the same way again.

THE RULES OF THE GAME

Treat this lesson as the rules to the game – your instruction manual. An important point to remember is that not everything you touch is going to turn to gold, every play won't be a home run or a David-Beckham-style free kick which sails into the corner of the net.

From the off, it's vital to note it's not a ten-step guide to making loads of dosh. There is no one-size-fits-all approach to never going broke, but we're going to give you the resources and as much insider knowledge as possible to make you successful.

It is more trial by error than a step-by-step guide. As time goes on, these errors will become less frequent. Go in with the mindset that not everything will be a success and you're going to encounter problems along the way.

The idea is that this is a low-risk strategy. We'll build you a pot of cash from seemingly nowhere and make you realize what value you have in particular situations. By the end, we hope to have showed you your particular strengths in the world of resale, strengths you had no idea you possessed before reading this book. If you fail at a certain trick, move on to the next thing – don't get too wrapped up in it.

Take multi-level networking schemes, also known as pyramid schemes, as an example. There is always this false pretense that if you fail, it's your fault, no one else's. The reality is you could fail because of reasons outside of your control.

Treat these failures as data-gathering experiences. For instance, you go to visit a charity shop and it has closed down. That's cost you time and money for petrol. But you'll learn for next time to check in advance and move on to the next thing. I am my business, and along the way, I have learned from my failures and successes. You'll be doing that, too, formulating and building your own mini business.

We are also all about mitigating risk and identifying the easiest opportunities. If you paid £10 for this book, we want to get you your tenner back ASAP. Everything else is then risk free – you're in it for nothing, as we'll make clear shortly.

You have everything to gain and nothing to lose, other than a bit of time and effort. Part I of the book is about building up a big, risk-free pot of money, in as simple and straightforward a way as possible. The hard work has been done for you – the money is simply there for you to go and grab like juicy banknotes hanging off a low-hanging branch. You can take advantage of each opportunity, or not. It's your choice.

It is also important to treat some of our ideas as passive opportunities. Sometimes the petrol costs outweigh the money coming in, but if you're already heading in that direction, great – milk that opportunity. What we're saying is, try to build most of the ideas in Part I into your ordinary day, maybe your lunch hour or evening strolls. For example, if you're going for a walk anyway, take a bag with you. See a discarded can on the ground as essentially a penny shining back at you.

The personal stories and anecdotes we share here aren't just for entertainment. They are real-world examples of how you can apply the method we're talking about and replicate what we've done in your own way. We never retell stories for their own sake. These are lessons to take away from real-life experiences.

Lastly, it's worth noting that we play fairly loose with pounds and dollars. Prices are quoted in dollars when we're explaining stories or events that have happened in the US, for accuracy reasons, but the two are relatively interchangeable.

WHAT TOOLS DO YOU NEED?

Essentially, you will need three things. They are:

1. The internet
2. A smartphone
3. A bank account or Paypal

Most of you will have all of these key items, but some may not.

The internet

When it comes to broadband, make sure you're not paying over the odds. Use a comparison website to make sure you're on the best available package, and check you haven't let a contract expire and are now overpaying. There's nothing worse than wasting money in this lazy kind of way. You may need to contact your supplier and do the classic haggle dance – that is, find a cheaper deal, then tell your existing provider you're moving to the lower-priced deal. More often than not they'll match it.

For those of you who don't have the internet, if you have a laptop, smartphone or tablet, you can use free wi-fi in many public places. If you don't have one of these devices, the library is your friend until we can earn you enough cash to buy one. Libraries usually offer a free computer to use as long as you're a member – which, again, is free. Aren't libraries great?

If you do have a device, but don't pay for broadband, the easiest option is to visit your local coffee chain. Both Lee and I usually go to a fancy coffee shop to work, but order a cheap filtered coffee. We like to look the part.

Alternatively, libraries (again) usually have good wi-fi connection which is free to use as long you're a member. Wherever you are, make sure the connection is secure.

Smartphones

In terms of a smartphone, you don't need anything too expensive: a basic, internet-surfing device will suffice. Some brand new smartphones can be purchased for as little as £70 but resale websites and high-street secondhand stores will have used versions for less than that.

It is likely that a relative, a friend or a friend-of-a-friend will have a device lurking in a drawer that they can give, or at least lend, to you in the short term. It's always worth asking. You won't be at a disadvantage if you don't have the latest, expensive, top-of-the range smartphone in your pocket – a secondhand phone is just fine.

Even if you don't have a mobile contract, you can use it to surf free wi-fi (see page 23) – it's an important tool for some of the upcoming lessons. It's also a handy way to keep an eye on your Never Go Broke pot of cash, by downloading your bank's app. Again, make sure the connection is secure.

Bank accounts

While most people have a bank account, or at least a Paypal account – or equivalent – some don't. In fact, around 1.5 million adults in Britain are believed not to have one.

If you do have one, make sure you're getting a good deal that might pay you a little bit of interest on your credit balance or choose one with a snazzy app that can help you segregate the funds you make from your resale adventure. Most banks, from names that have been around for decades to fintech newbies, now have incredibly user-friendly apps.

In fact, we recommend that you open a second current account solely for your resale purposes. You could try one of the new digital upstarts, which make it easy to see how much money you're making and prevent the temptation to dip into the pot and use it for everyday life, especially in the beginning. Only do this if you haven't recently opened another bank account, as you don't want to hurt your credit rating. Also, avoid accounts with an overdraft facility – that's when 'free' banking isn't so free anymore.

I am blown away by the banking options in Britain: in the US, there aren't many 'free' accounts on offer. But in Britain, banks will bribe you to switch to them. If you play the game properly, you can switch from one to the other, triggering bonuses – some even have friend referral schemes. That could put a few hundred quid in your account within 12 months. Not being loyal = free money. It's incredible. These deals chop and change all the time so research online to find your best new second home.

Think of banks like casual dating. Your status says, 'I'm looking to settle down'. But you're really thinking, 'I'm just looking for a fling until the next opportunity comes along.' Don't get married to your bank – they just want you for your money.

It should be relatively straightforward to sign up for a basic bank account, without the bells and whistles, if you don't already have one. You'll need basic ID, be aged over 16 and offer proof of address. If this isn't you, some apps will allow you to open an account online without a UK address, but you'll still probably need ID and access to the internet to open it. If none of these options helps, Citizens Advice may be able to steer you in the right direction.

ACTION POINTS AND KEY POINTS

Throughout the lessons, we have dotted in 'action points'. These are where, if you choose, you can stop what you're doing to perform a task that will help you on your Never Go Broke journey. This might be to put money in your pocket straight away, or to pause and research some of the points we're discussing.

There are also lists of key points. When you've read this book cover to cover, you can flick back through it and see at a glance those real key points to remember.

THERE'S NO TIME LIKE THE PRESENT

We are confident that this book will be the best investment that you've ever made and we want to see you making money straight away. The hardest part is getting started, so do the following now to see those pounds come rolling in:

1. Sell some things in your home right now (see page 32)
2. Take some surveys or get a few vouchers (see page 76)
3. Resell something (see page 119)

Share your stories with us on Twitter (@NeverGoBrokeUK) and Instagram (@nevergobrokeuk) and keep visiting nevergobroke.co.uk for more new inspiration and ideas.

LET'S DIVE IN

There, you've made some cash. You're chomping at the bit to grow your pot now, aren't you? We warn you, making money becomes addictive. Some of the tips may seem elementary at first but you'd be wise not to overlook any of them. Right. Stick the kettle on and pour yourself a cup of resale ambition. We'll wait…

Ready? Okay then, let's get started on our magical carpet ride of buying, selling and making money.

RESOURCES

Compare the Market (www.comparethemarket.com) – a
comparison website for broadband deals, insurance and energy
providers

Confused (www.confused.com) – a comparison website for
insurance deals and energy providers

GoCompare (www.gocompare.com) – a comparison website
for financial services, insurance, broadband deals and energy
providers

Never Go Broke (www.nevergobroke.co.uk/resources) – our pick
of the best broadband, mobile phones and bank account deals

PART I:

BUILD A RESALE POT FROM NOTHING

There is such a thing as a free lunch –
it just might not be caviar and Champagne.

In Part I, we outline five lessons to show you how to build up a risk-free pot of cash for your later game of resale. There is free money everywhere, you just need to find it and shake that magic money tree.

The first step is to find the free money lurking around in your home.

The second step is to find the free money other people and companies have and want to give away.

We'll talk you through how to sell all the items in your home that you no longer want or need. Do not simply assume it is junk that you cannot make money on. We'll also show you how to make easy cash from other people's laziness.

We'll reveal how to recycle your way into making money, where to find free cash lurking on the internet and how to sell the best asset of all: yourself.

This part will teach you that you can make money from nowhere and we'll make sure that little piglet bank grows into a plump piggy bank in no time, before we head off to learn your resale blueprint.

LESSON 1: SELLING ITEMS IN YOUR HOME RIGHT NOW

TARGET: RAISE £100 SELLING ITEMS YOU NO LONGER NEED
POT GROWTH POTENTIAL: ££££

Most of us are guilty of having far too much stuff knocking around our homes, whether it's in the attic, garage or crammed into nooks and crannies elsewhere. A new trend has emerged in recent years – the detox of the home and 'clean' living, meaning many people want their household decluttered. We'd argue there are a number of big reasons for this.

Firstly, social media – especially Instagram – has inspired many of us by showing photographs of clean-looking interiors without an item out of place. Just consider the popularity of Marie Kondo, the self-styled 'organizing consultant'.

Secondly, austerity and the aftermath of the financial crisis has made people more conscious of spending frivolously, alongside the economic turmoil unleashed by the pandemic.

Lastly is the mindfulness movement – a clutter-free home equals a clutter-free mind. Whichever of these you buy into, it's safe to describe the Western world as nations of hoarders coming off the back of an era of cheap goods imported from around the globe.

All of these items do, however, have value, whether they are old magazines or your first Action Man. For that reason, you shouldn't simply write items off and take them straight to the tip or give them away.

Take those two examples. Lee subscribes to *National Geographic* magazine. Some early copies can sell for big bucks, so they are worth keeping an eye out for, as many people have them knocking around their homes. They can be sold on the internet – not for huge money but definitely a few quid. One trick is to list them as '*National Geographic* for those born May 1976' or whatever dates you have. There is a market for people buying them as a birthday gift.

Meanwhile, Action Men? Those little plastic figures can sell for a few hundred pounds if they are in good condition and from the 1960s and 70s. See one at a car boot sale? Take a look at it carefully, then step away and try to establish how old it is online. An increasing number of 60s and 70s Action Man 'survivors' have fallen into collectors' hands, sparking a spike in price for those in good condition.

ACTION POINT: Download the eBay app, or bookmark eBay. It will be your new baseline price guide and personal appraiser to look up and gauge how much items have recently sold for and their value...and all for free.

PLAY THE POST-IT NOTE GAME TO SHARPEN YOUR EYE

Grab your smartphone and some Post-it notes (or even just some scraps of paper). Go into any room in your house, select half-a-dozen to a dozen items dotted around and write a rough price you'd accept for each on one of the notes. Now I want you to do some market research into each item you have selected online.

As you find the selling value, start sticking a second Post-it (preferably a different colour) on each item to compare the two. After you get the bug, do an entire room and add up the total value. Theoretically, you can do this in your whole home. How much is your total 'collecting net worth'? It can be a surprising amount.

Those long cold winter weekends are perfect for this, especially when you see the sum total of all the goods you have in your castle.

One of the takeaways of this lesson is this: I want you to be able to walk into a room and almost accurately put a price on every item contained within it.

Some people have athletic talents like LeBron James and Serena Williams, some can visually see music like Mozart and Kanye West. My special gift is I can walk into a room and put a value on everything in a space. I want to train you up to do the same.

Does it turn my brain to mush sometimes? Yes. But if you can ID the value of goods in a room, you can then transfer this skill set to other places, such as car boot sales or auction houses – you never know what you're going to find and make money on, and when that retained information will help.

It is hell-as exciting.

If everything has value and you treat it as such, you shouldn't write anything off.

ACTION POINT: Play the Post-it note game to find out the value of one of the rooms in your home.

USE MY SIMPLE TIER SYSTEM FOR SELLING

Complementing my Post-it note pricing is a tier system I always use; it works well when selling items from the home or from elsewhere.

- Your top-tier items should go to auction houses, antiques dealers or specialists.
- Your second-tier goods should be listed for sale online.
- Tier three is essentially your car boot sale items – stuff that you know will sell well at those events.

• Lastly, you have the bottom tier – essentially items that
  have a recycling value, like scrap metal.

The idea behind using this system is that you will never want to overlook anything, which is so easy to do. I've heard it a thousand times, 'It's not worth anything, just bin it'. But there is value hiding in every item. I'm telling you. It's how I continue to make a living doing what I do.

You can number each Post-it note with the tier you believe the item to sit in. For example, writing '1' for top items and circling it, right down to '4' for the scrap goods.

INCOME JAR

I have a simple concept I use called the income jar. When you're selling several items at a time, the total earnings may come to a random amount, like £2.04 or 57p. A prime example: I just sold a tonne of electronics that I had accumulated for £113.

With that odd £3, it's easy to write it off and spend it on needless consumables such as candy, beer, whatever. If you're in London, it's only going to pay for half of a beer.

But spending that £3 is akin to automatically writing off its potential simply because it's the 'extra'. In reality, it means I've made £110 and I'm blowing the other £3. However, when you start buying and selling more frequently, you're going to be making these odd sums more often and it adds up quickly.

I'm a pretty lacklustre spender and I don't follow every single pound of expense because I know I'd go crazy. I do, however, have a jar – basically a coffee can – and I put all my spare change in it until it's full.

The most important thing is to choose a container that you cannot see into because if you can see the money, the temptation is to take it out and spend it on rubbish. Have an income jar, keep it out of sight and out of mind, and over time it will slowly build up like a resale piggy bank.

Once it builds up, you're going to have stacked up a decent sum – a bonus resell gift if you will. This can be reinvested and the aim should be to double your money. In the lessons further on, we'll show you how.

It's also worth opening a separate current account and you can even fill up your income jar and deposit it into your account if you find that easier. It is surprising how quickly your piggy fund can mount up.

MULTIMEDIA: AN EASY PLACE TO START

Most of us have a large number of multimedia items in our homes. As technology has adapted, the need for CDs, DVDs and Blu-rays, for example, has been zapped by online streaming. Although, interestingly, vinyl and video games buck this trend – this is because those growing up in the 1960s, 70s and 80s now have plenty of disposable cash to blow on their hobby. We'll get onto this shortly.

Place one of these items in front of you – either a CD, DVD, Blu-ray or video game. Search for that specific secondhand item on Amazon, eBay and Google to see what it is going for. More than likely, it is going to have value. Quantifying the value is crucial. If you have a normal DVD, it is unlikely to be worth more than a quid – but some special editions, especially Blu-rays, can fetch a tidy sum. Once you've watched a DVD, one study suggests you are 70 per cent likely to never watch it again, so there is not much point holding on to it.

These days, with the technology on smartphones, it is easy to get an instant price for your items. We'd recommend downloading a handful of scanning apps. Using your phone and its camera, you download the app and scan the barcodes of CDs, DVDS, games, Blu-rays and even books, those dusty old ancient things you've been holding on to.

Within seconds, you can have the app downloaded and items scanned, instantly giving you a price. You box the items, they pay postage and packaging and you can have the money almost instantly in your bank account. Not everything has a code, but you can ID the majority of items quickly for an instant uptick in your finances.

What's most valuable? An expert at Music Magpie says, as a rule of thumb, the maximum it'll pay for a CD or DVD is around £2.50, or £15 for a video game. They add, 'Academic books tend to be a good money maker as they are usually quite expensive to buy new, and so the used market is strong and maintains prices.

'With media such as CDs and DVDs, it's the more esoteric titles that maintain value. Where the amount purchased by consumers as new is lower, this means the amount traded-in is also lower, and so the price tends to stay high.

'A lot of indie and metal CDs maintain value, but the same is true across most specialist genres.

'Blu-ray box sets and 3D films also tend to hold value well – this is particularly true of titles where sales haven't been high. In addition, recently released titles hold their value for the first year or so.

'Where a lot of product has been sold, the value drops quite quickly. The only exception to this are titles that are very popular – this includes media such as *Star Wars* and DVDs from *Marvel*.'

Downloading more than one app here is vital to compare prices. Often, it can be better to split your collections in order to make a few extra bucks. To highlight this, we scanned 17 items – a mix of fiction and non-fiction books, CDs, DVDs and Xbox 360 games.

Of the 17 items, only one CD didn't have a price on any of the three apps mentioned above. Everything else had value. The most valuable was a parenting book, followed by a 1990s copy of teen-lit *Point Horror*. But prices varied hugely.

App A offered the highest price seven times, App B six times and App C three times. That's a pretty big split and highlights why you should shop around.

For 14 items (removing the CDs here, as they weren't as valuable as other media) if we went for the highest bidder for each, we'd have made roughly £11. If we'd taken the lowest prices, it would have been around £4. If you scale that up – say 140 items – we could be talking £110 or £40 for the same items and effort, a £70 difference. If you did 140 items per month, that could be £840 of missed profits a year, for no reason.

I honestly become so upset when I watch television programmes in which people are struggling to pay debt, owe hundreds or even thousands, and I see all of this media in the background. I recently watched an episode of such a show and saw £300–£500 worth of mixed media in shot for a few seconds, using my mental Post-it note system. These items are easily sellable, but it is the same with so many other things.

You can use this barcode trick outside of the home, too, but more on that later.

ACTION POINT: Download three barcode apps and scan 20 items to see how you can get a price quickly and easily.

OLD VIDEO GAMES AND CONSOLES

I love retro gaming. It helped me start my resale career and I'm glad it did. I truly was – and still am – interested in the area. Many people will have old consoles gathering dust around their homes as they upgrade to newer, better technology – or because they have been ordered to by their partner.

However, people become nostalgic for their youth, especially in a time when video games have become so darn realistic. It means there is a huge resale market of people saying, 'God I miss so-and-so game, I'd love to play it again.' From Pong to Mario to realistic first-person shooters with graphics that are in 4K, the evolution has been speedy.

These days, some of the rarer consoles and handheld games systems can go for big bucks while even once-common ones can sell online for a tidy amount. The usual adages apply – the rarity of the system, its condition and whether it has its original packaging will massively swing what price you can get for it.

Furthermore, if you have a good bundle of games to go alongside it, the price will rise again – although sometimes it can pay to sell them separately. Do your research.

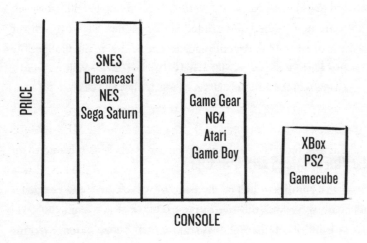

Sony PlayStation consoles are among the biggest selling of all time. In fact, the PS2 is the biggest-selling console ever. For this reason, they don't fetch huge money online. Usually no more than £50, if in good condition.

However, some once-common gaming systems can turn a tidy profit. You can split them into three categories. In the top tier is the Nintendo and Super Nintendo Entertainment Systems, and the Sega Saturn and Dreamcast. These tend to sell for the highest prices.

In the middle tier is the Nintendo 64, Game Boy, Game Gear

and Atari. In the bottom tier is the Xbox, PlayStation and Nintendo GameCube.

This is a rule of thumb, and there are some anomalies such as the Atari Jaguar which can sell for huge money. Additionally, if a console has its original packaging or is a special edition, it is likely to have extra value.

This also can be transferred to video games. For example, *Pokémon Blue* and *Red* Game Boy cartridges usually sell for up to £30. However, if they are new, sealed and graded 9.8 or higher, they can sell for upwards of £1,500. A decent place to check this is the Collectible Grading Authority, which will give you an indication of how good a condition a game is in – giving it a rating out of ten.

Video games are incredibly hot at the moment. How much do you think a sealed copy of *Super Mario Bros* for the NES sold for at an auction recently? Take a deep breath…$114,000. It sold to an anonymous bidder at a Heritage Auctions event in the US. It was graded A+ condition and had a rare variant on the game's original packaging: a cardboard hang tab rather than a plastic one.

In total, that Nintendo auction raked in $699,000 – around a third more than its estimate. A sealed copy of Mike Tyson's *Punch-Out!!* sold for $50,000. This highlights the money now in vintage video games and how it can pay to keep items like this in their original packaging.

Recently, I made contact with someone who had video games for sale online. When I turned up to take a look I discovered a Sharp television with an in-built NES in it. The seller didn't have a clue what it was worth, whether it worked and why it had just been gathering dust in her attic.

I knew it was rare because I am interested in the video game market and I'd never seen one before. It transpired that these were sold on shopping channel QVC and are one of the rarest pieces of Nintendo kit you can get. I offered her the entire contents of my wallet, around $250 and she was delighted. It transpires it is worth a few thousand bucks.

EVEN OUTDATED TELEVISIONS AND ELECTRONICS SELL

Lee tells me that he bought a new television recently, one of those with a thin line of casing around the screen, rather than the old chunkier versions. He already owned two the same size, but both had become a little dated and looked cumbersome. Vitally, he couldn't connect to Amazon Prime and Netflix content at the click of a button. Both were hand-me-downs, one from a friend and another from a relative.

The temptation was to throw them out, take them to the dump. Instead, he listed them on Facebook Marketplace. But who would want to buy an old television without high-definition capabilities?

It turns out, loads of people. Listed for £50 each, one Samsung and one Sharp, they both sold for the full price and were collected from the house by locals within hours of being posted. Cold, hard cash for something that could easily have been thrown out. It transpired that both of these televisions were destined for spare rooms where the buyers' children play computer games.

Facebook is actually not a bad place to flog items like this now. Meanwhile, apps like Shpock are also growing in popularity. If you don't list it, you won't ever know if anyone is willing to part with their cash for it. Small efforts can add up to good returns. After all, £100 on two hand-me-down televisions is not to be sniffed at.

It is also worth pointing out that era-based items can sell well too. Recently there has been a boom in popularity for 'retro' 1980s goods – think Walkmans and Boomboxes, and even fashion. We'll get into this in more detail in Part II.

VINYL CAN RESULT IN GROOVY RETURNS

Vinyl also falls into the same category as video games – older people hungry to recapture their innocent youth, listening to that beautiful sound of vinyl. It has that nostalgia factor. Furthermore, these people are hovering around retirement age with plenty of disposable income to blow on that old Pink Floyd album, which sounds much better on a record player than streamed on a modern device.

Collecting vinyl has become big with millennials, too, with a huge surge in reasonable-costing record players now available. This has amped up the value.

If you do come across a box of old vinyls and you have no idea what you have, it may be worth taking them to a specialist. That is because some vinyls that you believe to be common and thus not worth much could be rare copies or highly desirable. Furthermore, vinyls with mistake prints, such as words spelled incorrectly, can drive up the price.

Here are a couple of examples of valuable vinyl. Madonna's *Lucky Star* can't be worth much, right? Not necessarily. A 7-inch version was released in Britain in September 1983 and the Queen of Pop's second single only reached 171 in the charts. It was re-released the following March and hit the number 14 spot. But copies of that original release sell for huge money – up to £2,000 a pop.

Another example is *Diamond Dogs* by the iconic David Bowie. Common as muck? Yes. However, copies of the original release sell for big money. This features Bowie as half-man half-dog on the sleeve, which proved controversial. At an auction in 2014, a copy of this version fetched £3,700.

Outside of these rare anomalies, you can still receive good money on some vinyls that came out as CDs were becoming popular. For example, vinyl copies of *The Joshua Tree* by U2 can fetch up to £80 if in good condition because many more copies were sold as CDs than records. Mint copies of *Spiceworld* by the Spice Girls can go for £200, for the same reason. And, on this note, if an artist comes back into vogue, prices could surge higher. A good example of this is the Spice Girls and the publicity given to their 2019 tour.

Other huge albums – think original Beatles, The Who, Elvis and other timeless artists – are still highly collectible in mint condition. A good place to get values is Discogs (see the resources section on page 55).

One example is the Beatles album *Yesterday and Today*. There are two versions that, at first glance, look exactly the same. But one is worth a four-figure sum, the other a single digit. This is because hidden behind one of the sleeves is an alternative controversial cover that is rare. It's a first pressing and is known as the 'butcher album'. They sold hundreds of thousands of albums with the newer cover photograph and it can be identified by a 'Gold Record Award' red stamp.

Food for thought.

DON'T JUST BIN OLD CLOTHES

We're all guilty of buying too many clothes, cluttering the home. Around 350,000 tonnes of clothing goes straight to landfill each year in Britain. Furthermore, it is estimated that we buy 38 million items of clothing each year and throw away 11 million – fast fashion has become a dirty habit.

It is also believed that £25–£30 billion worth of unused clothes are sitting in our wardrobes in Britain – imagine just tapping a small slice of that.

Many of us bag up unwanted clothing, then throw them into one of those charity bins. I can guarantee you've wondered if your clothes really go to the charity printed on the side.

My wife Nicole and I have a vintage clothing business. It requires us to sort through piles of clothes to find a particular design, look, time period or feel, specific to our needs. A by-product of it is that we are given so many clothes for free. Bags of trousers, skirts, dresses, t-shirts and shoes. Naturally, the majority of these clothes don't fit into what we need and we're left with a tonne of clothes that aren't vintage and have little resale 'value'.

But, remember, everything has value – even if that value is minuscule. At one point we had 90kg of clothes with no idea what to do with them. But some companies will pay for clothes by weight. With the car filled to the brim, we drove to one at a nearby location on the way to another destination we were already going to, plonked the clothes on the scales and received 30p a kilo for them. Some high street shops will also accept your old clothes to turn into a voucher to spend in the store.

Although it is not a massive money-making opportunity, it can add up over time and most people will just throw clothes away. I do plenty of house clearances, especially when an older homeowner has passed away and their relatives want to sell the house and don't care about the contents. I'll come in and take everything inside, including clothes. All items have value.

Furthermore, Lee tells me that recently at a car boot sale he couldn't believe how popular clothes were. He had some worn football boots which were the first items to sell on his stall that morning. An old pair of women's roller-skates were not far behind.

He also says that he set up a clothes rail full of worn dresses from his other half and, again, these sold like hot cakes. They were all destined for the jaws of clothing bins dotted across the land. These weren't big labels (these are best sold online or via specialist shops). Instead, they were common high street labels such as M&S, Next and Topshop.

Again, this fits into my tier system. The top tier is your designers, such as Gucci, Prada and Max-Mara. The middle tier is M&S and Next, while the bottom tier is Primark and supermarket clothes. You get the gist. The top tier needs to be sold properly, the middle tier is fine at a car boot sale or perhaps online, while the bottom tier is most likely your 'scrap' clothing.

Lee said it was a similar story with a pile of t-shirts destined to be binned. He simply sold them for £2 a pop and shifted a dozen or so.

It is imperative to display clothes properly at these types of events – a clothes rail is a must for dresses and suits. Meanwhile, t-shirts and tops should be spread out, not stacked on top of each other, so people can see the designs without having to rifle through them. Later on, I will tell you how vintage clothes can pay for a holiday in California. Yes, really.

It is also worth mentioning that wedding dresses go for big bucks. Sure, they hold sentimental value, but you could get hundreds for them.

Additionally, many towns and cities have baby boot sales – essentially, it's where parents offload all the clothes, toys and baby equipment when their children have outgrown them, along with unwanted gifts. This is a great way to declutter and offload items you no longer require, which happens at a speedier pace when you have children.

Again, use my tier system when selling baby clothes. Brands such as Ted Baker and Joules are more likely to shift for good money than bargain-basement labels. A top tier exists here, too, with brands such as Baby Dior and Petit Bateau. Don't let nostalgia get in the way of making money, ready to make resale memories.

There is, of course, the option to sell clothes online – eBay will be most people's first port of call. Top-tier labels can sell for huge sums – this is what buyers are likely to be hunting for. Some middle-tier items will sell, but don't expect more than a few quid, depending on the item, while bottom tier clothing is unlikely to be worth listing.

Before choosing eBay, remember to check postage and packaging costs, and see if the same or a similar item of clothing you have is listed on there, for what price and how much interest there is.

If you want to take it a little more seriously, you could consider setting up an Asos Marketplace store. This will be for those who have a serious clear out on their hands, with good brands, or are potentially looking to go into buying and selling for profit, perhaps snaffling bargains at charity shops or abroad to make money. We go into more detail about this later on. Just remember, again, to check how much of a cut Asos will take. There are other similar online marketplaces worth comparing it to, such as Depop.

ACTION POINT: Have a small wardrobe clear out and pick some top- or middle-tier items – then see how much similar items are selling for online.

CRAP FURNITURE? NO, IT'S VINTAGE DARLING!

Another bulky item that many people simply think of as garbage is old furniture. Something that was stylish ten, twenty years ago may not be now, and you want to update. In many cases, with a bit of TLC, these items of furniture can be worth a pretty penny.

It is estimated that more than a quarter of a million tonnes of furniture is available for reuse each year in Britain alone. At an antiques market Lee goes to in Battlesbridge, Essex, there is a specialist shop that will buy your old furniture and upcycle it, then flog it for big money.

If you do have a bulky item of furniture you want rid of, make sure you know what it is made from – some woods, for example, can be highly sought after and expensive.

Other highly desirable furniture you can easily shift for cash is nursery furniture, such as cribs and storage. Having a baby is expensive and the secondhand market for this type of furniture is huge, especially via resale groups on social media websites such as Facebook.

Our current generation is guilty of living in a 'fast' culture and furniture is no different. The cost of goods on sale in shops such as Ikea means we can update our interiors to fit in with every passing trend. But there is a change afoot. Antiques research engine Barnebys, which monitors more than 2,000 auction houses, says secondhand furniture sales rose 32 per cent in 2018.

This surge in interest is said to be down to the under 45s looking to sniff out a bargain, usually to furnish their first home. And this means that old chests of drawers or cabinets could be worth a pretty penny. Many people who no longer want such goods will just smash them up and take them to the tip.

Furthermore, some of the most common things people put out on their front doorstep is free furniture. Awful, out-of-date furniture. But if you have the creative knack and energy for it, so many of these pieces require one minor update to become both modern and fashionable again: paint. A worn, nasty piece of furniture can look like a fresh and modern upcycled piece with a simple coat of paint.

A top tip for giving wooden furniture some shine and a lovely smell? I highly recommend orange oil furniture polish, which costs around a tenner a bottle. I bought six teak chairs at a house clearance for $300. I gave them a quick polish and sold them at a car boot sale for $1,000, with simply a touch of orange oil. It makes wooden furniture shine and in this case helped me more than triple my outlay.

Lee, at the aforementioned antiques market, snapped up a gold-effect drinks trolley for his home in 2016 for £30. Thanks to a surge in popularity since, many high-street shops are now knocking out similar replicas for £200–£300. He reckons he could get triple the price for it now.

Don't write furniture off. Trends come back around. Chin chin!

LET'S TALK ABOUT COINS, BABY

Lee won an award in 2018 as the inaugural coin writer of the year – seriously! There is not much he doesn't know about the UK coin market. He has even been given a private tour around the Royal Mint in Wales, thanks partly to the fact that he has been a huge driving force behind the recent boom in popularity of numismatics – coin collecting to you and I. He also receives dozens of emails a day asking to value people's coins.

There are a number of collectible coins you may unknowingly have rattling around. Lee wrote a story about it back in 2016 which went viral and has been read millions of times. Here are some prime examples:

Kew Gardens 50p from 2009. There were only 210,000 minted. These can now sell for north of £100 online. It features the pagoda in the middle of the coin with the years 1759 and 2009 either side.

Other 50p coins that can sell well include 2012 Olympics coins and certain ones from the Beatrix Potter collection, which can easily sell for 20 or 30 times their face value. One of the London 2012 50p coins can also sell for four figures online thanks to an error, which collectors love. Before the Olympics, the aquatics coin – depicting a swimmer underwater – was redesigned by the Royal Mint to make the swimmer's face visible. But before the change was made, an unknown small quantity of the coins with the face masked with lines were made. Those can be worth £1,000.

There are mistakenly undated 20p coins from 2008 that can sell for more than £150 online, while 2p coins from 1983 that say 'New Pence' can sell for more than £500. Meanwhile, the rarest 50p coin is the 1992/3 EC Single Market design – it's the old style, heavier 50p piece. These can sell for huge sums online.

If you have a piggy bank full of coins, or a special pot of coins that you've kept because of the design, you should check online to see how much they are selling for. One word of advice here though: do not believe that because a certain coin is listed for a certain price, it is worth that. Check actual selling prices – the coin is only worth what someone is willing to pay for it.

When collectors have taken certain coins and kept hold of them, it's driven up the price. For example, it is believed that 75 per cent of all London Olympics 50p coins aren't in circulation now, making it harder to get one in your change.

As a rule of thumb, the lower the mintage and the more that have been taken out of circulation, the more valuable the coin. All those listed below (excluding the Judo and Football 50p) have been minted fewer than a million times:

Angel of the North 10p	rough value if sold online: £4
Tea 10p	rough value if sold online: £2.50
Kew Gardens 50p	rough value if sold online: £100–£120
Judo 50p	rough value if sold online: £8
Football 50p	rough value if sold online: £10
Edinburgh £1	rough value if sold online: £45
Northern Ireland Commonwealth £2	rough value if sold online: £30

Additionally, many of us have euros rattling around at home after adventures on the Continent. These are worth investigating. Back in 2002, for example, 7,000 Italian one-cent coins were struck on two-cent blanks. These can now sell for thousands. Yes, thousands.

If you have old European currencies – Deutschmarks and Pesetas for example – you can take them to Fourex machines dotted around train stations in Britain, to turn into sterling. It's an easy way to exchange old, now-defunct currency into cash.

Lastly, remember when the new £5 and £10 notes came out? Lee was the reason why you were checking the serial numbers on the notes – he realized ones starting AA01 and AK47 were being sold for hundreds of pounds online. They still go for a small profit online, but nowhere near the price they were going for at the beginning of that craze. It's a classic example of a popularity bubble and boom.

Later on, we'll reveal how we bought a bathtub of old coins and spent a day sifting through it for profit. I'll also reveal why I bought a £5 note for £1,200. The things we do for money. Literally.

ACTION POINT: Check your piggy banks, jars and sofas for coins – anything that looks slightly unusual, put to the side and then hunt down its value online.

MUSICAL INSTRUMENTS SELL WELL

The best-selling pre-loved category on eBay is musical instruments, with cellos and clarinets proving popular, according to data from the online marketplace in the run-up to Christmas.

In order, the rest of the top 10 are: vehicle parts and accessories, cameras and photography, antiques, books (along with comics and magazines), business and office items, sporting goods, computing and networking, garden and patio items, with sound and vision in at number 10.

HOME DECOR – LIPSTICK ON A PIG

You are likely to have put your own personal touch on your home. Everywhere you look, your style is staring back at you. It's unlikely you have Andy Warhol or Picasso prints on the wall, more likely those lesser-known artists Dunelm, John Lewis and Wilko. However, as life moves on, so does your style and personal tastes, and that could create a whole heap of home decor and seasonal or themed items that you might no longer want. Trends come and go.

It is likely you have plenty of items – from lamps to cushions – that you do not believe have value, quite possibly gathering dust in the garage or loft. Home decor should be the last priority in terms of trying to make money selling items from your home. But let's say that you have Christmas decorations you no longer want as you have changed style for that year. I would say rather than trying to sell items piecemeal, just bundle them up and flog them in a box at a car boot sale or on Facebook Marketplace.

When you're sitting in your room, all you see when you look around, just by turning your head, is nothing but home decor. It is potential money right in front of your face but it might be a case of putting lipstick on a pig. That is, you might need to be creative to create value when it's not necessarily there, by presenting it in a unique way. It's the same when you're buying antiques that look unappealing – you clean them up, make them look better, take excellent photographs. I'd much rather buy a pig with lipstick than one without.

I'd always recommend working on a bundle. For example,

kitchenware. You wouldn't sell individual forks, knives and spoons, but selling an entire – or near entire – set will have value.

While you may have decided that your leopard print room had to go and is now a zebra print room, there will be plenty of people ready to pounce on those leopard-themed goods. People love to find these secondhand bargains, whether it is in an antiques store, car boot sale or online.

Lesson I summary

Always assume everything you have has value...EVERYTHING. It may not, but at least you've done your due diligence, learned potential values, and didn't risk throwing away a huge potential score all because you discounted a treasure.

If you do one thing?
Find 10–20 items in your home you're willing to part with, research their potential value and sell the most expensive.

RESOURCES

Never Go Broke (www.nevergobroke.co.uk/resources) – go here for our pick of the barcode scanning apps

Discogs (www.discogs.com) – a music database

Cash For Clothes (www.cashforclothes.org.uk) – a company that will pay money for clothes and other items in bulk

The Royal Mint (www.royalmint.com) – for coin mintage figures

Fleur de Coin (www.fleur-de-coin.com) – for euro coin mintage figures

Change Checker (www.changechecker.org) – for benchmark coin pricing

Coin Hunter (www.coinhunter.co.uk) – for benchmark coin pricing

Barnebys (www.barnebys.co.uk) – a search engine for art, antiques and collectibles

KEY POINTS TO RECAP

- Work out your home's net worth. Stick Post-it notes on items in a certain room or your entire property with your value on each, and then research the true value.
- Use this experience to tot up the value of items you see elsewhere, such as car boot sales.
- Use a tier system to know what item should be sold where – from auction houses to scrap centres.
- Start an income jar. Have a physical pot or account to build up a resale piggy bank.
- Sell your multimedia. Quick apps will let you scan barcodes and send a box off for easy hard cash.
- Vintage video games and consoles are becoming more sought-after and could boost your coffers.
- Don't throw away old, working electronics – there is often an easy secondhand market for these.
- Music can be worth a fortune, especially vintage vinyl – research before you're tempted to ditch it.
- Sell unwanted clothes. Use a tier system to sell items online or at car boot sales, or receive money-off vouchers from stores or scrap money.
- Don't write furniture off. Style is in the eye of the potential buyer who may be after a refurb project.
- Check piggy banks and behind the sofa. Some coins can sell for much more than face value to collectors.
- Home decor styles come and go, but don't write anything off. Even if your artwork is more Dunelm than Picasso.

LESSON 2: CARPE LAZINESS – MAKE MONEY FROM PEOPLE'S APATHY

TARGET: RAISE £50–£100 WITH FREE FINDS
POT GROWTH POTENTIAL: ££

Most of you will have heard the Latin motto *Carpe diem*. It translates as 'seize the day'. My version is Carpe laziness – seize and capitalize on other people's apathy.

It is incredible what you can achieve by simply putting in a little effort and going one baby step further than the average person can be bothered with. In this lesson, I will give you some simple secrets to make the most of bone idleness.

This is the whole embodiment of what I do – taking advantage of others' laziness and unwillingness to put in the time. I like to get dirty, tag it, bag it and make a profit. It's in my blood. I will honestly get down on my hands and knees and sift through bags to find treasure.

Many think I am some sort of appraisal expert. I am, but it is purely based on information that is accessible to everyone. Below, I reveal my simple secrets and say this: anybody on the entire planet can do the same thing. All I do is move in when people miss a step to put extra wonga in my pocket.

I have got so many great deals that anybody could have got if they'd invested one to three hours of their time. Anybody could have turned the same profit.

SWOOP ON YOUR NEIGHBOURS, FAMILY AND FRIENDS – AND THEIR FRIENDS, AND THEIR FRIENDS...

Here is a common example of laziness: people moving from one home to another and leaving behind big, clunky items that they cannot or do not want to take with them. You should take advantage – when you see a neighbour moving, swoop in like the beady-eyed resale vulture that you are (or are about to become). You can usually grab great items for next to nothing, or indeed for free.

These won't be rare antiques but everyday items on which you can often make £10, £20, £40: something for nothing.

One of the most common ways people are lazy is by simply loading up a car with items they don't want anymore and taking it to the local tip. There are hundreds of these across Britain. Some of them are now even setting up shops nearby, selling goods that have been dumped but have resale value, with staff keeping a look out for items that will do well.

I find that crazy. Don't let that be you. Go one step further, by either stepping in if friends, family or your neighbours want items gone, or even finding out where these shops are to snap up some real bargains to sell on elsewhere for profit.

You can literally build a car boot stall out of other people's goods and may even find some items that can sell for a pretty penny online. Friends, family, neighbours – they don't want to sell and don't have the time, inclination or energy to get up first thing and get stuck in.

Always be open and mindful of when people want to get rid of their stuff. It's a secret business without you even realizing it.

THIS TIP IS A LITTLE TRASHY

I'm warning you now, this next tip is a little trashy. But it is one of my favourites and, when it comes off, it fills my beating resale heart with joy.

I'll often head to the communal apartment bins to take out the trash. When I do, I take a quick peek inside those huge bins – they can be akin to metal treasure chests. I have taken loads of stuff from the bins, from a bird cage to a branded beer bucket, and turned them into £10 or £30, an instant online sale. Super-easy stuff. Not only are you a winner, but you'll save the environment – it's only going to end up in landfill otherwise.

Another good spot to do this is the car boot sale, and it is another perk of going at the end. For many people, this is the 'last stop' before they put their leftover wares in the skip or donate to charity. So look in and around the bins at car boot sales at the end of the day. I have found vinyl, crystal, art and electronics this way, which I have sold on.

Granted, it does feel a bit extreme. But money is money. It's a matter of rolling up your sleeves, grabbing the item, giving it a five-second wipe down and selling it at another car boot sale or on eBay. It is a great feeling getting even, say, £10 for free. I always find myself (slightly) fond of that item, too, when selling. I want to see it go and have a second life. Money for trash.

There is a seller I know in my local antiques mall called Kathy. She has made $50,000 in the last few years solely by finding freebies to sell on. It's truly inspiring.

In a similar vein, another seller I have met in recent times is a man called Ken. He goes to car boot sales, prices everything at $1 for the last hour and sometimes then just says everything on his stall is free for the last 20 minutes.

I turned up once in that last period of time and said I'd take everything for a nominal fee. It was tools and garden decorations mostly. They needed a little cleaning up, but there was value in them. The next time I went along, he let me have a look at his items before he put them on sale. I ended up taking 75 per cent of what he had in the back of his van; I cut a good deal.

It turned out to be one of the best resale moves I've made and highlights the importance of contacts as you're about to find out.

ACTION POINT: Close your eyes and think about the most valuable thing you have ever thrown out. Why did you do it? What would you do now to sell it? And how much could it potentially be worth now? Get a bit cross with yourself and vow never to do it again.

HOUSE CLEARANCE

I have made some serious profits doing house clearances in the US over the years. It happens in the UK, too. You'll often see vans roaming around offering to take anything off your hands – they'll go in and do a house removal, with the proviso that they get to keep anything they find, while clearing out the trash.

While this might seem like quite a professional road to go down, if you know of someone who needs a house clearing and you're at a loose end, it can be a route worth exploring. Often, people seem to miss a trick here. They gain ownership of a home with a pile of items in, often through inheritance, and simply get a clearance company to come in and take it all away.

What you could be doing is turning up and saying, 'I will pay you money if you let me rummage around for items'.

Ken, mentioned already, saw I was a serious buyer after that second visit and asked if I would be interested in helping him with a house clearance. My dad and I went along, but it ended up not being any old clearance. It was four homes over 20 acres with more than a dozen sheds. We offered the seller of the property a couple of thousand bucks to clear it out but take what we wanted.

It was hard work, but there was so much cool stuff there from the 1940s, 50s and 60s, including a 40s Ford tractor and four ride-on lawnmowers, which more than paid our outlay back straight away. I even found a 5150 IBM computer in the study that I sold for $500, and dozens of cement statues that I sold for $60 a pop.

You may be reading this and muttering, 'Jesse, you fleeced them'. Reader, I didn't. The children who inherited the estate ended up selling it for $5million and, other than a few sentimental items, just wanted it all cleared in a month.

Two other cool items I found were some original bricks from the old building that was there (I've kept hold of them – literal rubble) and near the end our time there, a huge hole filled with trash. Do you know what that hole transpired to be after I cleared it out? An abandoned silver mine. I just didn't have the time or tools to explore further.

FREE FINDS

Quite often, a scour around your neighbourhood on an evening stroll can also prove fruitful, with many people leaving items outside with notes saying, 'Free, take me!'.

When I see items discarded in this way and they are in good condition, I can't help but scoop them up and attempt to sell them on for a profit. Even if I find just one item a week and sell it for a tenner, that is £40 a month or £480 a year from simply finding stuff people no longer want in their front gardens. Crazy.

Lee tells me that in one week he managed to snag a Little Tikes slide which he had almost bought for £50+ for his daughter, along with a working Hetty Hoover for kids and a great lamp in pristine condition.

Once his daughter grows out of the slide, he's going to list it online to make some money on it. This is a great feeling – a free item that is saved from landfill, is used for a few years and can then be exchanged for cash for the future. All he had to do was lug it three minutes home.

He also recently saw someone take a free armchair in good condition in his neighbourhood. With a bit of upholstery work via a Youtube tutorial and some cheap raw materials, you could be talking some serious profit.

It is also worth looking on Facebook Marketplace and Gumtree for these free finds. You'll be surprised how desperately people want to ditch stuff to make space.

ACTION POINT: Check local marketplaces for items being handed out for free and go for a stroll to see if there are any goodies in your neighbourhood. Then put a value on them.

LAZINESS IS EASY TO EXPLOIT

In Parts II and III you will come to realize just how easy it is to take advantage of people being lazy and not marketing items correctly, or simply deciding that an item doesn't have much value. It can also be down to desperation. Some of the common scenarios are moving home in a hurry and not having the time to properly sort through all the items amassed over the years, or wanting simply to be rid of clutter quickly, without bothering to take the time to make money. We will be encouraging you to take advantage of these easy wins.

Take another house clearance example. I paid a man $60 to clear the house that belonged to his dad. He wasn't bothered by profit at all, just wanted it all gone. That $60 turned into $2,000 with little work. It turned out his dad was a rock collector. While there was nothing that precious, there was quantities of the stuff, like ammolite and jadeite.

In a later lesson I'll reveal that it's not just everyday folk that become lazy in this way, businesses can too. This resulted in me bagging a $6,500 profit, just by asking some questions about an item at a zoo. Just call me the profit penguin.

Lesson 2 summary

If you are prepared to put in a bit of extra time and effort, there is plenty of free stuff waiting to be turned into profit. Cash in on the laziness of others.

If you do one thing?
Scour your local area, preferably on foot, and try to find a discarded item that you could flip for a profit, or do it online.

KEY POINTS TO RECAP

- Help people moving out by offering to take any items off their hands they're not taking with them.
- Do a car boot sale with all the free finds you get from doing the above – it's money for almost nothing.
- Don't be afraid to get dirty to rescue items destined for landfill. Make it your aim to sell them on for a joyful profit.
- See if you can help do a whole house clearance. I've made huge money doing this, but it can be hard work.
- Look out for items in your day-to-day life that can be sold for a profit – making it part of your daily routine is an easy way to start.
- Laziness is one of the things I exploit the most. Always keep that in mind.

LESSON 3: RECYCLE THE WORLD – CASH FOR TRASH

TARGET: RAISE £20 BY RECYCLING
POT GROWTH POTENTIAL: £

With a bit of TLC (Tender Loving Creativity) you can make money from your recycling. This lesson is not only good for your pocket but also for the environment. With an increase in concerns over the future of our planet, this trend will only continue to grow.

Upcycling old, tired items from around your home rather than chucking them out – giving them that TLC – could result in a nice bit of profit. When you see items like this, things that are broken, damaged or simply old, no matter what they are, they will have value – and there are plenty of tutorials online to show you how to fix old things.

Also, if you're constantly putting your empty drink cans into the recycling bin, stop. You're giving away money. Seriously. And armed with an inexpensive litter picker, you can make money from items discarded thoughtlessly on the ground outside the home.

Here we reveal how you can make money from discarded items, from mobile phones to your luscious locks.

ALUMINIUM CANS

Councils will take your recycling, sift through it and make sure it is being properly taken care of. It's much better than it heading to landfill. They also make money from some of it, such as aluminium drink cans. They won't get much and the profits help offset other costs, but that is money that could be going into your resale pot.

Many countries around the world, including the US, offer money for recycling cans at special centres, with recycling values varying from state to state and in Europe. Some charities and schools do this in Britain, but you can too. It won't make you rich, by any means, but it will help keep that pot of cash ticking upwards.

There are more than 500 cash-from-cans locations across the UK, where you can exchange your aluminium cans for cash. The best way to do this is to build it into your everyday routine. Let's say you walk the dog. In that hour walk you could take a backpack with you and manage to find 10 cans. That means 70 cans in a week, alongside any your household may have consumed. But let's stick with 70. That's 280 cans a month. Let's say you collect them in a garage over the course of the year, so you now have around 3,000 cans.

Make sure they are alucans – with an alu mark and a shiny bottom – and crush them to make sure they don't take up too much space. Around 60 cans make up a kilogram, which will sell at a cash-from-cans centre for around 30p–50p. You'll get less if you want the company to collect them from you.

Your 3,000 cans will weigh around 50kg, that's potentially £25. No, not life changing. But it's good for the environment and can become a bit of an obsession, a hobby to keep stacking up those kilos of cans. I recently took a haul in while in the US and came home with $57.25 in my pocket. You can ask friends, family and even neighbours to save them up for you. Get creative. It's money for trash.

MAKE-UP AND CLOTHES

Other examples of money for trash include returning old make-up packaging to some companies who will, in turn, send out free cosmetics. Some retailers also encourage recycling of clothes and textiles. They pay around 30p–50p per kg for unwanted garments. In some cases, customers can return unwanted clothes from any brand in any condition and receive a 10 per cent discount voucher on their next purchase. Others offer loyalty points. But be careful doing this – sift through for top-tier items and make sure it is only the real basic, cheaper labels that go this way, otherwise you're giving up cash.

MOBILE PHONES

How many of us are guilty of upgrading to a new mobile phone and then leaving the old one to gather dust in a drawer? It's time to sell them – ideally you will start getting rid of your old ones straight away to maximize their resale value.

Some companies will allow you to cash in the phone as a deposit to put towards the cost of a new one. If you didn't do that, you can flog the old one on eBay – people are always after cheap mobile phones. And, hey, you might be helping out someone who needs one.

You should compare the prices you could be offered on the high street and on websites. Shop around, flip the role on its head and sell to the highest bidder, not just the first company that comes along. Again, it might not be huge sums, but it will all add up.

This goes for other tech that you no longer use. Music players, stereos, computers, headphones – they all potentially have resale value. Just because you no longer use them doesn't mean there isn't a market for them.

ACTION POINT: Locate all of your old phones and electronics, and establish a total resale value for them all. (Don't forget to delete all of your personal data first!)

EMPTY INK CARTRIDGES

You can earn up to £1.50 for posting on used and empty ink cartridges. Many people take them to the free recycling bins in supermarkets, but why let the grocery giants cash in?

There are specialist websites that will take them off your hands – but check the details. Some will only take certain brands such as Brother, Canon, Epsom and HP, and they might also need to be an original cartridge and not a refill.

Again, it could be worth asking friends, family and even neighbours for theirs and become their point of call for recycling these things.

LET GO OF LEGO

You can gather up old plastic Lego that is no longer being used and recycle it for cash. It has to be the official stuff and in good condition. By doing this, it doesn't go to landfill and it will be recycled to be made into something else. If you have family and friends who have tubs of the stuff, you could ask to take it off their hands.

Be warned though: if you have complete Lego sets, check how much they sell for online and in local marketplaces, as it is likely they will fetch far more.

DON'T LET BUILDERS TAKE YOUR COPPER

If you have work done on your property, your builders may try to take away the copper. A common example is when undertaking a loft conversion. It may seem like they are doing you a favour, taking it away and replacing the pipe work, but it all has recycling value.

You could get around £3,500 a tonne for copper wire, £3,200 for copper, £3,000 for brazier and £2,500 for brass. Furthermore, you can get £600 for aluminium, £600 for stainless steel and £1,200 for lead. It's worth bearing in mind.

Let me shoehorn in another tale here about scrap prices, too. Recently, I was walking home from the supermarket when my eye was drawn to something lurking in the mud. I picked it up, it was an earring that clearly had been there for some time and I was fairly certain it was gold. I took it home, cleaned it up and took it to three different shops who 'pay cash for gold'.

The first shop confirmed it was 9ct gold and would pay me £8. The second offered £10. Both of these are high street names you'd recognize. The third, an independent shop, said £15.

This gives you two lessons. Firstly, always keep your eyes peeled. You never know what discarded 'junk' you can find on the floor. There's a man in New York who claims to make $500 a week collecting fragments of gold and jewellery from the city's pavements. Secondly, always shop around for the best price for anything, especially in a circumstance like this where all of the shops are all within a few minutes' walk of each other.

RECYCLING DEFUNCT COMPUTERS

If you have old electronic equipment that no longer works, it could be possible that it has scrap value. I know someone who makes money stripping out circuit boards from old laptops and PCs, cutting off the fingers because they're made of gold.

You can also find circuit boards in other consumer products such as mobile phones, bluetooth speakers and televisions. The gold bits look like little piano keys. Gold is used in these products because of its conductivity and resilience.

If you have old laptops or PCs, it is well worth taking them to a local specialist to see if they have scrap value.

OTHER RANDOM ITEMS WORTH CASH

Websites such as eBay, Gumtree and Preloved are full of strange listings, including recyclable household items such as jam jars and wine bottles. People will buy these items for crafting projects. Jam jars and ramekin dishes have also become a popular way to create decorations such as candle holders for parties and weddings.

Sold prices on eBay suggest you can sell 30 jam jars for around £10, 10 glass ramekin dishes for a fiver and 50 green plastic milk carton lids for a fiver too. Even old perfume bottles can go for up to a tenner, depending on the brand.

Meanwhile, reverse vending machines are now being used to boost the recycling of used plastic bottles. These pay out 10p for each bottle deposited. And even old corks from wine bottles can be saved and sold – people will buy them online on sites such as eBay, to use them as placeholders at weddings or help make their own corkboard for their kitchen. I kid you not.

The hair on your head is also worth cash. No, I haven't gone mad, it's true. For those lucky enough to have ever-growing luscious locks, you can sell unwanted hair for a bit of extra cash. It is recycled to make wigs. You can easily find websites that will buy it and you send it to them in the post – hair mail.

UPCYCLING TREND

As previously mentioned, upcycling furniture can be a way to turn profits. Lee recently rescued an old cabinet that was part of his mum's house clearance. She had no room for it in her new downsized property, but they couldn't bear to get rid of it because it was the last thing they owned belonging to Lee's grandparents.

It was a bit scratched, but the quality of the wood was excellent. Lee decided to sand it down, buy some copper paint for a few quid, watch a tutorial online and give it a new lease of life. He'd intended to sell it on, but has decided to keep it for now as it looks nice in his dining room.

The moral of this story is that you should think along the same lines. Lee isn't a dab hand with DIY or an upcycling expert but it still turned out great. Don't just trash dated items like this – find their value.

It's not just furniture. Britain has gone wild for television shows such as *The Repair Shop*, where people bring in old items that may no longer work – think antique watches, jewellery, furniture and the like – which have a back story and are then given another lease of life.

While a specialist is needed to do work on intricate, unusual items, there is no reason why you cannot roll up your sleeves and tackle some simple ones yourself. Challenge yourself to find a few unloved items, perhaps buried in your loft or garage, and give them bit of TLC. Then list them on Facebook or eBay, or take them to a car boot sale and try to turn them into cash. It is rewarding and it will help build this resale pot we're working towards.

Lesson 3 summary

Think what you can recycle instead of throwing away. It's good for the planet and can be good for your wallet.

If you do one thing?
Gather up all old, unused mobile phones and use an online resale website to get some cash.

RESOURCES

The Aluminium Packaging Recycling Organisation (www.alupro. org.uk) – to find local aluminium scrap dealers near you

Think Cans (www.thinkcans.net/cash-cans) – tips on can recycling

CeX (uk.webuy.com) – a high street retailer for selling mobile phones

Envirofone (www.envirofone.com) – a website for selling mobile phones

Music Magpie (www.musicmagpie.co.uk) – a website for selling mobile phones and Lego

The Recycling Factory (www.therecyclingfactory.com) – a website for selling old ink cartridges

Cash for Cartridges (www.cashforcartridges.co.uk) – a website for selling old ink cartridges

Ink2U (www.ink2u.co.uk) – a website for selling old ink cartridges

KEY POINTS TO RECAP

- Get cash for cans – it won't make you rich, but you can stack them up as part of a daily routine.
- Recycle clothes – items that cannot be sold on individually can be sold in bulk.
- Mobile phones – check those drawers and sell on old phones for a small cash injection.
- It's a bit of a hairy one, but you could sell your locks.
- Empty ink cartridges can be sold for cash. You can become a centre for your friends, family and neighbours to leave them (along with their cans).
- Recycle your Lego – it's better than it ending up in landfill or you constantly treading on it.
- Scrap metal: know the value as you don't want to lose out on an easy win.
- Random items can be worth cash, including jam jars and wine bottle corks.
- Upcycling won't be for everyone, but with a little TLC, you can add value to most items before selling them on.

LESSON 4: SIMPLE WAYS TO SCOOP 'FREE' CASH ONLINE

TARGET: RAISE £50–£100 WITH FREE ONLINE CASH
POT GROWTH POTENTIAL: £££££

One of the easiest ways to fill up your piggy bank while dedicating just a few hours a week is through the magic of the internet. But how can you make cash out of nowhere online without being scammed or potentially giving up all of your personal information?

Unfortunately the internet is full of scammers, so you will need to be on your guard. And when it comes to your own personal information, you'll need to decide just how far you're willing to go to make some quick money – don't give up any sensitive personal data, and read terms and conditions carefully.

Some of the ideas below will require some patience but, ultimately, can lead to free money for essentially very little. None of it is going to make you minted, but it could help you not go broke and also build up that pot for bigger, better things. Think of it as a very skinny piggy bank that you are slowly filling up and remember, you don't need to do all of the suggestions. Pick and choose the ones that fit best with you.

SURVEYS

The internet is littered with survey websites, which will pay you (usually) in cold, hard cash for filling in questionnaires, although sometimes payment may come in the form of vouchers.

Some of the key things to know about surveys is that most of the websites will have a minimum payout that you'll need to reach before the reddies hit your account. The surveys will vary in length and they will be after differing demographics, so it might only be a slow trickle of surveys you can be involved in. This is very much a case of slowly, slowly catchy monkey.

We've listed some of the best places to start in the resources section at the end of this lesson – there are some well-known organizations along with a handful of lesser-known ones.

CASUAL CRYPTO

Now, cryptocurrency isn't for the faint-hearted. We have seen big price fluctuations and plenty of scams come and go. For this reason, please treat this segment with extreme caution and skip it all together if you simply know it is not something you're interested in.

Many people will have the shutters come down when you start talking about blockchain, Bitcoin alternatives and how it all works. I'm not going to attempt to explain it here, it requires a whole tome in itself.

What I want to tell you about is a way to get free crypto, that's legitimate, which you can then flip into Bitcoin without exposure – casual crypto for those who don't care about its intricacies.

Lee would like to point out here that he is bombarded with emails each day about cryptocurrencies and Bitcoin from over-eager PRs, company bosses and the like. They claim, among other things, that Bitcoin will replace gold as a safe haven within a generation and it'll be worth £100,000 or even £1million a coin within a decade.

We don't have a crystal ball. It's hard to predict what will happen tomorrow or next week, let alone in five years' time or an entire generation. But that doesn't have to stop you being involved, with minimal exposure. This, again, comes with a huge caveat – only do this if you're confident online and realize that Bitcoin is not a failproof financial instrument.

Firstly, I recommend downloading Brave browser. Simply put, it's a built-in ad system where you can choose how many pop-up adverts you see in a day, blocking out all the rest of the advert noise. It was created by the man behind JavaScript and the former chief executive of Mozilla, the company which developed software such as the Firefox browser, so it does have credibility.

You surf the internet as usual, and it then returns a crypto called BAT – Basic Attention Token – each month. You can convert this into Bitcoin using a crypto exchange. Or if you like, keep it as BAT.

While this is pretty simple, there are a few things to be aware of. You'll need ID to open an account with an exchange and some banks won't let you transfer money to cryptocurrency exchanges. There is also a raft of authentication to go through, AKA levels of security, and it can cost to send money back to your current account.

That aside, you will then have a pot to put your BAT coin into. Additionally, you can watch quick education videos on some exchanges to obtain other cryptocurrencies, which you can cash out of (if you choose) at a later date or convert into Bitcoin.

I've earned around £3 of BAT a month using this method, which I then convert into Bitcoin. This could easily be more like £8–10 per month for a typical user, depending on how much you go online.

Now, when I mentioned this to Lee – someone who has written plenty about cryptocurrencies in recent years – he wanted to be absolutely clear of the pitfalls of Bitcoin – namely, stick to the above and have no exposure of your own money, unless you are fully aware of all the risks.

Research from the Financial Conduct Authority – the UK financial watchdog – in 2019 showed that nearly two million Britons held Bitcoin. Just remember that money isn't protected like it would be in a savings account at a bank or building society.

APPS

There's a combination of things you can do with your smartphone and apps to make money. They can all be downloaded to your smartphone via Apple's App Store or Google Play Store. We'll start with another huge caveat here. *Please do your own research and do not download anything that looks remotely dodgy.* Due diligence is required. We cannot jump through the page and hold your hand.

Some of the ways you can be paid with apps is by performing day-to-day tasks and playing games. In terms of day-to-day tasks, mystery shopping is one of the best examples and simply requires you to photograph and document certain things while out and about.

For example, a brand of fizzy pop might request you go into a supermarket or local corner shop, photograph where it is in the shop, its position on the shelf, how much it is and how much stock there is left. You will get paid for this, in drip-fed amounts like the surveys.

Other examples we've seen include taking photographs of job listings in shop windows and taking photographs of household receipts and uploading them. There is a huge list of these types of app so we can't name them all – but we've mentioned some of the best ones in the resources section at the end of this lesson.

In terms of playing games, I'm going to give you one example: the Tetris app. It has a feature called Tetris Primetime that, at the time of writing, gives away up to $5,000 of prizes each night, worldwide. I love Tetris – as does Lee. We played in our youth on the Game Boy and were reminiscing about it recently.

Each night you can play to win. It gives out prizes if you're in the top 5,000 players (although it is worth pointing out rules can change and so can the prizes). In one month, I managed to earn £30 playing a game I love, and for free. There are other examples of this, and the list chops and changes, but the premise is the same. You are essentially competing to win the prizes, funded by advertising revenue.

I'd expect this trend to grow in the coming years – a blend of esports mixed with games people enjoy, and can easily take part in – so keep an eye out.

In a similar vein, there are websites that will pay you to do various tasks – such as making web searches or watching videos – and other internet browser extensions that will pay you for seeing adverts online.

EASY JOBS FROM HOME

Working from home has become the norm for some of those lucky enough to keep their jobs after the recent economic turmoil. Jobs that advertise as easy to do from home with huge hourly rates could be a scam so, again, due diligence is needed.

That said, sometimes firms will advertise jobs when they need repetitive tasks done that can be easily performed with a laptop at home. Some specialize in tasks such as proofreading, undertaking research, text creation, copy editing and checking the internet to see if certain websites need to have an adult content warning.

There are other examples of these types of website, which are for different skills and will require a varying degree of tests to 'get in'. For example, one allows you to test websites with your microphone switched on and potentially the camera too – but only if you pass a test to make sure you'll be vigilant enough to do it properly.

CASHBACK WEBSITES

These are immensely popular. Simply put, companies pay cashback websites money for each new customer they bring in, and the cashback website scratches your back by giving you a slice of money for going through them. .

This can be an easy way to stack up some cash for buying items you were already going to get. Just make sure you clean your website cookies or use another browser, turn off adblockers and read any offers you're signing up to carefully.

Additionally, they offer money for getting quotes on comparison websites, or signing up for free trials. This can essentially mean free cash for doing very little and some companies have low cashout rates, meaning you should be able to get the money, no matter how small the amount. It is easy to scoop £5–£30 quickly this way.

All of the above may sound too good to be true, with companies and apps giving away 'free' money. This is a popular misconception. Much like supermarket loyalty programs, many of these companies, especially newer tech start-ups, are valued by the amount of users. So offering a 'small' incentive to sign up potential new customers adds value to their business as a whole. It's up to you if you want to take advantage of these opportunities.

PERSONAL FINANCE PRODUCTS

It is entirely possible to get sign-up freebies for personal finance products, but you'll need to play by some rules and make sure you're not doing anything that can potentially damage your credit score, or put you in danger of running up debt. You need to play the financial big boys at their own game.

While some of this might not be direct ways to get free cash, it could help you save money on your bills. Lee loves personal finance and could bend your ear about the magic of compounding, the importance of a pension and all the rest, but this book is about resale and saving money.

Here are five quick-fire ways to save or make money:

1. Switch your main current account. If you've been loyal to the same

bank for a long time, ask yourself why. You could bank £150 pretty quickly just by hopping current account provider.

2. Energy bills: are you on a fixed-tariff deal? If not, why not? Make sure you always shop around each year – simply input your postcode into one of the many comparison sites available.

3. Loyalty doesn't pay and this is especially true of the insurance industry. Make sure every year you know exactly what you're paying for your car, home and travel insurance, question any rises and threaten to leave with better quotes.

4. Mobile phone users who let their contract roll over after they've paid for the device, you could be overpaying by £50 a month simply by not switching to a SIM-only deal on the device you now own.

5. Put 1 April in your diary. It is April Fools' Day, but also a date many telecoms giants, mobile operators, utilities firms and others put up bill prices. Have an audit before this day to try to dodge these rises and save your money.

With these savings, you could choose to put what you've saved in your pot for your later resale adventure.

ACTION POINT: Think about how long you have been with the same bank. Is it time to try somewhere new? Have an audit of your finances. Are you paying the best possible price for your energy, insurance, mobile phone, broadband and other bills? Any money you potentially save can be diverted into your resale pot.

DISCOUNT CODES

When it comes to buying something you were already planning to buy, on top of trying the cashback websites mentioned above, make sure you are hunting out discounts. There are a number of avenues to do this and it astonishes me that not everybody does.

If a shopping basket has a little box to enter a promo code, it is likely there is a promo code out there somewhere in the digital ether. A quick search for discount codes online will spurt out a number of websites potentially offering you a percentage off, but just make sure the links you are clicking on are genuine.

Also try visiting the social media channels of the brand or website you were going to buy from to see if they have any offers – many will have first-time customer offers. If you have already used one of these, get a friend to sign up with a different email address on your behalf to get the discount for you again.

Load the item(s) into your basket and leave them hanging for a bit. Go make a cup of tea or browse some other websites. There is a chance a web chat will start, and it could offer you some money off to entice you to complete the purchase.

Another trick that can work is to copy the item code – say a television make and model – and paste it in your search engine to see if it is cheaper elsewhere. Sometimes this will prompt a discount or, at the very least, a price match.

More often than not, you can find coupon codes that save you 10–60 per cent off a purchase. The game here is to take the money you've 'saved' and put it into that all-important resale piggy bank you're going to want for Part II.

Lesson 4 summary

If you know where to look, there is money to be made online through completing simple tasks like playing games or taking part in surveys. Bigger profits can be made by saving money on bills and purchases through cashback websites, discount codes and price comparison.

If you do one thing?
Spend one hour per day for a week and make it a game to see how much online cash you can scoop.

RESOURCES

Ipsos Mori (social.i-say.com/) – a survey website

Opinium Research (www.opiniumresearch.co.uk) – a survey website

Yougov (www.yougov.co.uk/join-community) – a survey website

Prolific Academic (www.prolific.co) – a survey website

Survey Network (www.surveynetwork.co.uk) – a survey website

New Vista Live (www.newvistalive.com) – a survey website

Valued Opinions (www.valuedopinions.co.uk) – a survey website

VoxPopMe – a survey app

Never Go Broke (nevergobroke.co.uk/resources) – go here for more info on crypto

Roamler (www.roamler.com/en/crowd) – an app where you can perform easy tasks for cash (you'll need an invite, which can be easily obtained on its social media pages)

Storewards – an app where you can send in pictures of receipts for cash

Swagbucks (www.swagbucks.com) – an app where you can earn points for making web searches, watching videos or completing surveys. You can then convert this into vouchers or cash

Gener8 (www.gener8ads.com/products/ads) – an internet browser extension that pays you for watching adverts

Clickworker (www.clickworker.com/clickworker-crowd) – a website with quick proofreading, research and copy editing work opportunities

What Users Do (www.whatusersdo.com/file/how-become-whatusersdo-tester) – you can test websites with your microphone and camera for cash

Quidco (www.quidco.com) – a cashback website

TopCashback (www.topcashback.co.uk) – a cashback website

Never Go Broke (nevergobroke.co.uk/resources) – our pick of the best bank accounts, energy, insurance and mobile deals

KEY POINTS TO RECAP

- These aren't ways to make big money – rather ways to slowly fatten up your resale piggy bank.
- Surveys can be worth it: find the ones that'll pay you in cash and have plenty of opportunities to participate.
- Cryptocurrencies – only get involved if you want to and follow my two simple steps to avoid any exposure.
- Use apps to earn money for day-to-day tasks and potentially for playing games but due diligence is required.
- Make money doing jobs from home, with your own skill level to help build your resale pot.
- Cashback websites – sign-up to them and earn easy money for performing everyday tasks.
- Give your personal finances a regular review to make sure you're saving as much money day-to-day as possible.
- Discount codes – not a way of making money, but saving it for purchases you were already going to make. Put the difference in your pot.

LESSON 5: SELL YOURSELF! MAKE MONEY FROM YOUR TALENTS

TARGET: MAKE £50 SELLING A TALENT
POT GROWTH POTENTIAL: £££

In the last lesson of Part I, we are changing tack slightly. So far we have given you easy ways to get cash scores to build up an important resale pot; this one is more down to the skills and talents you have – how to exploit them for cash. Now, before you get any strange ideas, we're talking above-board stuff here – more arts and crafts than S&M.

We live in an age now where you can sell anything, from items you create or music lessons online to handyman/woman services that you can do in your local area. We'll point out, however, that you can only sell a talent if you have what is needed. Tarquin from Surrey is not going to want piano lessons online from someone who can only play the *Eastenders* theme tune.

We'll give you inspiration as to how to make some extra cash if you're currently out of work – or some ideas for a side hustle if you have a job but want to build up your resale pot a little further.

Meanwhile, if you do find yourself out of work, we have some tips for you on how to get by and, with a little social engineering, you can potentially bag yourself a job by simply showing a little enthusiasm to get ahead of the competition. It can be that simple (but not always).

POCKET MONEY BASICS 2.0

These are tough economic times for many, with jobs being axed and roles hard to come by. Lee was recently telling me of a qualified engineer who took a delivery driving job and that he was really enjoying it. He doesn't want to do it forever, but it's keeping him ticking over for now while he regroups and refocuses. He's plugging the gap.

The majority of you will know how to make money in your neighbourhood with very few tools. It is likely you did one of these types of jobs in your teenage years: dog walking, babysitting, washing cars, cleaning homes or even becoming a local tour guide, all for a little pocket money.

These small jobs have been rebooted in the dawn of the app and internet, where good reviews and safety are key. They also make connecting to the right people simple. Essentially, these jobs have evolved from a teenage pocket-money earner, to pro level.

Want to do some dog walking or sitting for extra cash? There's an app for that where you can connect with pet owners looking for the above and you can create a profile. A few good reviews and you'll get more business. There are also apps for babysitting, car washing and cleaning.

What we're trying to say here is that these simple pocket-money ideas have moved into the 21st century and can be an avenue to explore. Whatever you'd like to try, there's probably an app for it.

Meanwhile, the internet has created an easy way to cash in on other talents you may have that might fit your skillset better...

WEBSITES TO SELL YOUR WARES

These ideas could earn you some extra cash from the comfort of your own home.

Perhaps you have unheralded knowledge and experience in a certain field, and you can upload tutorial videos – this can be done onto a website such as Youtube to coin in some advertising revenue. If you get good and obtain a following, you can start to sell courses on specialist websites.

These courses could be for teaching languages, a musical

instrument, poetry or yoga. The internet makes the world small, and people around the world could be interested in your area of expertise.

Just make sure that you can make professional videos – there are many free tutorials to teach you how – and that you have enough expertise in what you're teaching. It's no good teaching French if you can't speak it fluently and can barely get by on your C-grade GCSE. It won't work.

In a similar vein, you could tutor on Skype – for example, when school exams come around, parents will be hunting for good tutors who can engage their kids and help them pass.

Even university students may be willing to pay for some help, someone to help them develop ideas for essays or dissertations – or even just to proofread their work. We're not talking about writing it for them, but helping guide them into finishing it, especially if you have first-hand experience.

If you have a creative talent, you can make and sell wares on specialist craft websites. You can set up a virtual shop. The best-selling shops are those that sell unique jewellery, party supplies, clothing, vintage items, art and posters. There are many unique and unusual routes you can go down. You need to find your niche, whether it is knitted goods or painted baby dolls rescued from charity shops. It's all on these websites and it could all potentially sell.

Other websites offer freelancers the chance to list digital services such a logo design, voice overs, digital marketing, video and animation, writing or translation. Others allow accountants, lawyers and other professionals to potentially make money, or to answer questions – although you may well need qualifications for this, especially for IT, law and medicine.

There are hands-on websites that link people looking for help with specific tasks in a local area with those that may be able to help them.

This can include putting up shelves, lifting heavy furniture or building those pesky Ikea wardrobes that people snap up, and then get in a tizz over when they see the instructions. If you are handy like this, you can register and be vetted. It could help boost your income – especially in the evenings and weekends.

Another option is to approach small, local businesses and offer to do their social media for them. This might not be the easiest sell, but if you have the experience and a way of backing up claims for boosting business this way, firms may be willing to pay you a monthly fee for posting on Facebook, Instagram, Snapchat or Twitter for lead generation. Again, if you do a good job, this could help build a portfolio and lead to more work.

ACTION POINT: List the talents you believe you could potentially make money on. Then hunt down apps and specialist websites you might be able to use. Don't feel like you have a talent? You do! Visit the government careers website and find free training that could help pave your way to learning something new.

YOUR CAR CAN BE THE STAR

Another simple way to plug the gap is to use your vehicle, if you have one, to get work. Before I delve into this, I'll say that you must have the right insurance cover and factor in costs such as depreciation and petrol.

Delivery jobs have boomed recently – you simply turn up at a warehouse somewhere in your vehicle, are loaded with parcels and given a route to drop said items off.

The boom has been down to more households choosing to order goods online. Lee has been getting his grocery shop from Morrisons supermarket recently, delivered via Amazon Prime Now, by delivery drivers who are just ordinary folk in their cars needing the work.

Other car options include becoming an Uber driver or contacting a local taxi firm. Some companies also offer the chance to stick adverts on the side of your vehicle, potentially paying you £100 per month, depending on how much you use the car and the routes you take.

ACTION POINT: Think how you might make use of your car for cash. This is widely regarded as the newest untapped opportunity out there. From rideshare apps to car advertising placements, there are also new apps that allow you to rent your car out for others to use. Take a look around the app store and a quick search online for new opportunities using your vehicle.

YOUR HOME – THE COMMODITY

There are a number of ingenious ways you can turn your home into a big brick piggy bank. You could:

• Rent out your driveway for cash. This works especially well if you live near a train station, sports stadium or other popular venue. There are a number of websites you can do this on now, and some people make thousands of pounds a year doing it. (Lee did this in the summer of 2013 when he lived in a home near Wimbledon tennis ground. For the two-week duration of the tournament, he and his housemates made £60 per day.)

- You could list your home on a location agency to rent it for filming and photo shoots for cash.
- If you are lucky enough to have space in a garage, loft or even spare room, there are specialist websites where you can rent it out to those who need it. It's a win-win, as it'll be cheaper for them than renting a commercial unit, and you'll make some extra money that can be used for your resale adventure. Yes, you can pimp out your home for cash.

FIXING BROKEN ITEMS – A NEW SKILL?

There are plenty of handy people out there who can repair items. You can give them a broken piece of electronics, a broken video game system, a broken car and they'll say, 'Hey, I'm a mechanic, I can fix this thing'.

If you become good at repairing items you can pick up for peanuts, there's an opportunity for you to put in a little elbow grease to flip that baby and make a little bit more profit. But don't get hyped up on the items – use your own insight and knowledge to ask yourself if you are able to make it better. If not, do you know someone who can and how much do they charge?

You can ask them if it's worth your time buying a broken video game machine for £100. How much would they charge you to fix it? And then you compare your costs with the price you think you can sell it for.

If you go on any high street now you'll see a mobile phone repair shop. It's a cottage industry that has sprung up because people smash screens all the time. Fixing phones is actually an easy skill to learn: go on YouTube and type in 'how to fix an iPhone screen'. The parts cost next to nothing and people make a load of money doing it – either repairing phones for people, or repairing old broken ones they find to sell on, just because people don't have the time, effort or inclination to fix them themselves.

It doesn't mean you have to get into the mobile phone repair business, but it's an example of what people are doing after watching just one YouTube video. This is interchangeable with all manner of other broken items. It could be worth focusing on one area, so in the future if you spot a broken item for sale, you'll know how much it'll cost to repair, the time required and the potential resale value.

Want to monetize your talents one step further? Many people film their expertise to teach others on YouTube. Even if it is something small or niche, you can make money this way like tonnes of people already. For example, I once needed to replace the icemaker in my fridge, so I did it myself to save money by watching a repairman on YouTube. His video had over half a million views and he had over 100,000 subscribers, just from filming himself repairing a fridge and other appliances.

ACTION POINT: What could be your smartphone fix business? Take a look around your home for inspiration and then find a relevant YouTube tutorial video – and perhaps find inspiration to create your own series of 'fix' videos.

JOB HUNTING IS SIMILAR TO RESALE

If you are out of work and are eager to get back in, no matter what the role is, there are some simple mistakes that people make when trying to get a foot in the door.

While *Never Go Broke* isn't an employment guide, we do have some strong contacts when it comes to recruitment and I believe in many ways, it's very similar to being successful at resale. If you're trying to look for CV tips and formatting or interview questions, this is not the place to do it. There is plenty of help out there.

What we're talking about here is how to sell yourself by being creative, different and using social engineering tactics – whether you're at a car boot sale, trying to land a £100,000 job or looking for your first role, the skills are the same.

I always think about the story I heard about an employer going through a stack of CVs – one of them was printed on pink paper. It really stood out.

Personally speaking, I recently hired someone at the family antiques shop, not because they had a CV crammed with the right experience, but because they had the right attitude. When sending their CV through a recruiter, they were the only applicant who filled in a personal message box. What it contained wasn't some extreme or bold way this person was going to change resale. They simply put, 'I like your antique mall, I like antiques and I'd be a good fit as I'm interested.' That's it. I called them in, made sure they had the same enthusiasm in person and hired them. I didn't even check their CV. So many people fail to make even little enthusiastic steps like this.

Lee started a series called the Interview Cheat Sheet years ago, which gives a number of top tips to make sure your CV is good, your covering letter is tailor made for the role you're after and offers interview help for those who need it.

One of the key things to remember, especially in a time of job uncertainty, is that many people are going after the same job. Don't be disheartened by this, just let it inspire you to make sure you're at the thin end of the wedge. Do everything in your power to bag a job by setting yourself apart in a positive way, establishing enthusiasm and clearly showing you've researched the job and company.

Whether you're researching a dusty old antique in a car boot sale, or that £100,000 job, you want to set yourself apart by speaking up and being proactive, but also knowing what you're talking about. Don't be another CV in the stack, set yourself apart by putting in that research and effort, finding the value in that job and understanding what it is and what it's about.

It's also worth pointing out that many major companies have a robot that filters out any CVs and covering letters that don't make the grade, so you'll need to watch out for spelling and grammatical mistakes. Take your time and ask a trusted person to take a look at any documents you're sending before you do.

Lee points out two basic mistakes that people make time and time again:

1. Failure to read instructions. At school, Lee was told about a test in which all pupils sat down and were told to read the instructions carefully. The instructions on the first page told pupils to read through the entire test first, from start to finish. The back page read, 'Don't fill anything in'. Only one pupil passed because they didn't answer a single question.

   It is still an important lesson and Lee has carried it with him for life, whether it is applying for jobs or trawling through terms and conditions. Read what an employer wants carefully and make sure the covering letter and CV fit accordingly, to beat those robots and get through to a real-life human.

In terms of resale, this is like blind-buying an item without doing any research. You wouldn't and shouldn't do it.

2. Talking yourself out of applying. Lee once visited a major bank that was running a programme for veterans to help get them back into work, outside of the usual security roles offered to them. Someone said their job in the army was as a sniper, then asked if they should avoid putting that on their CV.

A fantastic question; first of all you'd be forgiven for thinking, of course it shouldn't go on the CV. This person was a trained assassin. How could that fit into a normal office job? However, the recruitment expert said that roles like a sniper actually have a number of desirable job traits for an office. They include split-second decision making, risk assessment, confidence, analytical thinking, communication both one-on-one and as a team, discipline, planning, professionalism and dedication – all desirable skills in a 'normal' working environment.

What this shows is that all experience can be relevant. Don't write it off. In terms of resale, this is like pigeonholing yourself and turning down profit opportunities.

ACTION POINT: After a new job? Call a local recruiter and state the following: 'My name is... and I am eagerly looking for a new job opportunity. I am hard-working, flexible and punctual. Do you have any entry-level jobs that start immediately?' This is not a promise to get you a job, but more of a social exercise to see what job offers are out there you may not have known you could get or are qualified for. Remember: job recruiters are paid to fill positions, not embarrass or judge you. You can't get something if you don't ask.

Lesson 5 summary

Think of the resources you already have around you – your talents, your house, your car – and consider ways you can make money from them. If you are looking for a job, use the same skills to sell yourself as you would for any resale venture.

If you do one thing?
List your talents and then find somewhere – either physically or online – to make some quick cash from one of them.

RESOURCES

Rover (www.rover.com) – platform to offer dogsitting services

Sitters (www.sitters.co.uk) – platform to offer babysitting services

GoWash (www.gowash.co.uk) – platform to offer car washing services

Bark (www.bark.com/en/gb/cleaners/) – website to offer cleaning services

Etsy (www.etsy.com) – website for selling crafts and vintage items

Udemy (www.udemy.com) – website where you can offer courses

Skillshare (www.skillshare.com) – website where you can offer courses

Fiverr (www.fiverr.com) – website for offering freelance services

Upwork (www.upwork.com) – website for offering freelance services

Just Answer (www.justanswer.co.uk) – website where you can answer questions for cash

Task Rabbit (www.taskrabbit.co.uk) – website where you can list general handyman work

National Careers Service (nationalcareers.service.gov.uk/find-a-course) – government website with free training courses

Car Quids (www.carquids.com) – website for getting advertising put on your car for cash

Your Parking Space (www.yourparkingspace.co.uk) – platform to list a parking spot for cash

Just Park (www.justpark.com) – platform to list a parking spot for cash

KEY POINTS TO RECAP

- Go back to basics. Don't be too proud to get out there and make a crust – people will always want cars cleaned or dogs walked.
- The internet is your friend – there are loads of ways to sell your talents online.
- Tutorials can be an easy way to start on YouTube, or try private lessons on Skype.
- Get creative: you could set up an online shop selling things you've made.
- Software jobs can be posted online.
- Expertise could be needed to answer questions.
- Handyman jobs are readily available.
- Make money utilizing your vehicle.
- You could make money from your home, such as selling a car parking spot.
- Can you fix an item? Could you learn a new skill?
- When hunting for a job, be enthusiastic and dodge those common traps.

END OF PART I

Okay, we've reached the end of the first part of this book. We're hoping that you're now in the process of snaffling a lovely little pot of cash and the piggy is putting on some weight.

You will have noticed that we had targets for each lesson. There is no hard-and-fast rule, but if you've followed the tips, you could and should hopefully have bagged £100 or more within a few weeks.

If you've gone well above this, well done. If you haven't got close, it doesn't matter. It's not a race. Take your time and do it right.

We'd recommend going back over the quick recaps of each lesson before diving into the next part, which is going to teach you how to get into resale. There is plenty of time to keep working on your pot.

PROGRESS REPORT

Month	Lesson 1	Lesson 2	Lesson 3
1	£	£	£
2	£	£	£
3	£	£	£
4	£	£	£
5	£	£	£
6	£	£	£
7	£	£	£
8	£	£	£
9	£	£	£
10	£	£	£
11	£	£	£
12	£	£	£

Lesson 4	Lesson 5	Rolling total
£	£	£
£	£	£
£	£	£
£	£	£
£	£	£
£	£	£
£	£	£
£	£	£
£	£	£
£	£	£
£	£	£
£	£	£

PART II
LEARN YOUR RESALE BLUEPRINT

'Everybody that is successful lays a blueprint out'
– Kevin Hart

Now we've started the process of building up a pot of cash, it's time to teach you your own personal resale blueprint while those reddies stack up. These are the core concepts that I have used in my everyday resale life for the best part of 20 years and they've helped shape my buying and selling habits.

First and most importantly, it is essential to recognize that whether it is 1p, £100 or £1,000, absolutely everything has a monetary value.

Add to this the importance of carving out a niche, buying items you like and not chasing huge profits – at least not right away – and you're halfway to establishing your blueprint.

We'll also get you to focus on working out your 'hourly wage', seeing how and why contacts are so vitally important when it comes to increasing that wage, and the types of trends and patterns to look out for as you become more confident.

You will take the lessons you've learned here onto Part III, where we show you the places where you can put your blueprint into action and make some profits.

There is a notes section at the end of this part so you can jot down blueprint ideas as you go along (if you want to), see pages 183–5.

LESSON 6: STARTING FROM SCRATCH – EVERYTHING HAS VALUE

Everything has value.

'Really, everything?' we hear you cry.

Everything!

This lesson is one of the most important to remember when it comes to resale and it could be what separates you from the rest. It is essentially looking around and putting a quick value on everything. Remember that Post-it note game from the very start of Part I? This is the next step.

The first thing to do is visit Amazon or eBay and search for this book. Go on, do it. How much will you make by selling the book in your very hands? We told you it was good.

This is a mantra to follow, no matter what, and it is an important point to remember – your junk is another person's treasure, even if you really don't believe it is.

Did you know that some people sell cardboard toilet roll tubes and used underwear online for actual money? See, I'll say it again, everything has value – even if to you it doesn't. The world is open for business – there are around eight billion of us on this planet – and the internet has made people in New Zealand and Morocco markets for each other. There are no barriers.

Just don't think too hard about why the aforementioned goods are frequent sellers online…It's too late, isn't it?

'BORING' CAN EQUAL £££

A key thing to remember is that 'boring' items can be an untapped market for making money. This is because many people may not bother to find out about them. If it doesn't have the sparkle or excitement factor, the majority think it is not worth their time. I can tell you it is. Here's an example from a few years ago when I was living in the US.

I would sometimes do house clearances. This is where you clear out all the rubbish from an old garage or home, usually for free, with the proviso that you can take what you want from the clearance. I was clearing a house in a sleepy Californian town. Inside the garage was a dusty shoebox. The sort of unassuming box you could be tempted to bin without really investigating. Inside was what looked like funny miniature burnt-out light bulbs.

At least 98 per cent of people would think they were trash and I wouldn't blame them. I decided they might just be 'something', using my knowledge and the simple habit of not chucking items away because they look like junk. I loaded them into my truck and gave those little bulbs a chance.

At the end of searching through my haul – a frustrated pirate without any decent treasure from the clearance – I turned to that shoebox with little hope. A quick bit of research online revealed the bulbs are used to power now-defunct radios and also that they weren't burnt out. There is a niche market for those old radios and because these tubes (called valves in Britain) are no longer made, they have become hard to come by and, thus, collectible.

I'd seen many items in the past, but never radio tubes. Using the simple principle of 'everything has value' I'd luckily taken them home, even though I didn't think they were that valuable and had probably been overlooked by people for years.

Why was I lucky? Well, as well as bagging them almost for free – other than a few hours' work clearing a garage – I discovered they were Western Electric tennis ball radio tubes. It transpired that in working condition, these bad boys were worth $300 a pop. I had 24 of them. They all worked.

I had no idea they would be worth that much and I almost threw out a shoebox worth a small fortune. I had no perception of the value. All I had in mind was this principle, my own equation if you will:

$$VALUE$$

$$=$$

$$PROFIT\ MARGIN$$

$$X$$

$$RATIO$$

Now, having an equation might seem a touch Albert Einstein, but I assure you it is not. It is the basic equation I constantly have in mind when going about my day-to-day buying and selling.

My profit margin in this example is $300 per bulb (as I had no significant outlay) x 24 (the number I had) = the huge value those old tubes had, $7,200.

This equation is constantly on my mind when looking at items. It's on in the background, as I try to figure out whether it stacks up. The lesson to take from this? It is worth the time to investigate the price rather than toss out a potential gold mine – you never know.

Don't be afraid to learn something new…even if it is obscure, lame or boring. Because sometimes boring = serious money, as my bulb win shows.

Here's another example: I bought a storage unit and, much to my displeasure, it was full of Depression glass, which in a nutshell is old American dinnerware from the 1920s. The items were set to become my new targets at the gun range. However, I took my time, remembered the bulb experience and undertook some research. They transpired to be cups and saucers worth nearly $20,000.

Was it worth brushing up on my knowledge of the value of Fire King Jade-ite citrus juicers versus Anchor Hocking cameo green butter dish lids? I'll let you be the judge. I'm just glad I didn't stick bullets through them.

VALUE = PROFIT MARGIN X RATIO (CONT.)

Nearly everyone collects something, even if they might not realize how much that something could be worth to somebody who wants it. Some people collect rocks, others collect houses. Personally, I collect nothing, but like to tell people I collect money – I simply 'rent' collections then pass them on.

Research suggests the most popular items to collect, in rough order, are the following: comics, porcelain and glass, toys, shares, timepieces and scientific instruments, film posters, maps, classic cars, cameras, books, sporting memorabilia, coins, Art Deco, Victorian, vintage fashion, ethnic, militaria, nature-themed items, photos, music, high-end stereos, film props, stamps, autographs, diving items, sailing, horse riding and printed ephemera. This is an eclectic mix and it varies from country to country.

The last word on that list – ephemera – is from the Greek word meaning 'lasting one day, short-lived'. These items tend to be transitory documents created for a specific purpose and intended to be thrown away. Some collectible ephemera are advertising trade cards, airsickness bags, bookmarks, catalogues, greeting cards, letters, pamphlets, postcards, posters, prospectuses, defunct stock certificates and tickets.

In 2020 I started collecting free casino-branded facemasks still in their packaging. Why? Because there is an outside shot they could be worth some money in a few years' time thanks to the pandemic and scarcity. It's a rare example of a no-risk gamble from a casino. See, everything has value.

Sorted by value, the top three collectibles are classic cars, militaria and books. Billions upon billions of pounds are traded each year in these categories – and others that don't even make the list, such as radio tubes.

Let's take another example. If you walk into a garage and there is a Ferrari inside, you know it is going to be the most valuable thing in the garage. But going back to my equation and the profit margin, it might not necessarily be the best item to focus on. You need to look around and spot the untapped gold – or, to take my analogy, silly looking bulbs.

Anyone knows a Ferrari is likely to be worth big bucks. But this is where the true value comes in: you need to cross-relate it to profit margin. So, is it worth your time buying a Ferrari for £999,000 when it is worth £1million? That means a 0.1 per cent profit. And that's if you can find a buyer easily – you need to factor in the time it could take. It could be an expensive racing red elephant that you'll feel under pressure to shift.

Or, would it be better to spend £10 on an item and turn it into £100 – that's a 1,000 per cent profit and it is certainly less risky. See, value = profit margin x ratio.

HOW I MADE $42,000 ON A STORAGE CONTAINER

Blind bidding on storage containers can be one of the biggest thrills ever – but believe me, there is plenty of disappointment too. In the US, you can bid on the contents of self-storage containers that the renter hasn't kept up on payments for, or has been uncontactable, perhaps dead or simply moved state. Britain has speciality events in a similar vein and I'll tell you how to get involved later on.

For every ten containers, nine are likely to be full of real junk. Everything does have value, but if you've spent $1,000 to get the contents, there is a real chance you won't make your money back. It can be risky.

I have been pretty good at spotting the treasure-laden containers and avoiding being burned by the duds. My biggest profit on a single container was $42,000. Converted into sterling, that is basically the UK average wage for a year.

The container cost me $1,500. Why did I bid on it? Well, I simply saw one box that had a camera etched on it, around ten more marked 'Camera accessories' and another, near the back, that I could make out said 'Depression'. I simply connected the dots and decided it was worth buying.

It transpired that the container's contents included vintage cameras and Depression glass. I didn't know anything about either when I bought it. But now I know everything about Nikons, Polaroids, Kodaks, Canons, Leica – you name it.

Here's a fun fact: Leica collectors are mad for the cameras. Once on BBC television show *Antiques Roadshow*, a man turned up with a Leica and it transpired that he'd owned it for 45 years and it was one of only four made. It was initially valued at £5,000. A decade later, it went up for sale and sold for £320,000. That highlights the importance of popularity and scarcity, which we'll get onto in a later lesson.

I have retained bits and pieces of information about cameras so now, five years later, I can go to a car boot sale and if I see a camera I once owned in that collection, I can make a rational decision about whether or not I can make profit on it.

I spotted a Leica camera at a car boot sale recently and turned a 600 per cent profit on it when I sold it online. I simply had that little bit of knowledge that the brand, and particularly that model, are incredibly popular. The seller didn't know its true value and I took my chance. It was an open goal.

Having that information is amazing – it is based on a decision I made half a decade ago. You can make sure you don't go broke with simple ideas and retention of information. Real-life circumstances you're going to experience will be usable in the future – I have done this and I'm enough of an expert on a number of collecting categories to make a living.

I've had my fair share of failures, including some from storage containers, but I now have enough knowledge to avoid most of the pitfalls. This book is about laying out a baseline to hit the ground running. You'll make mistakes – but our aim is to keep them minimal.

FREE MONEY AT THE BANK (REALLY)

Banks know interest rates, but do they know – or care – about the silver content of their coins? Here's something I do from time to time to make a little bit of extra pocket money and it's ridiculously simple (and doesn't involve sifting through a bathtub of coins like Scrooge McDuck).

In the US, banks will change money for rolls of coins, a service mostly used by small businesses for change and whatnot. Any coins that are pre-1965 have silver content in them. I've gone in, handed over

$1,000 in notes and asked for $500 in quarters and $500 in dimes. I'm exchanging $1,000 for $1,000 so it's not costing me anything, other than a bit of effort lugging those coins.

People assume it's a burden I'm taking on because I'm left with all these coins. In reality, I take them home, slice open the rolls and identify any dimes or quarters that have any silver content in them. For example, half dollar Franklin coins, dated 1948–63 are worth at least ten times their face value, as are 1964 Kennedy ones (although these ones can sell for upwards of $15 online, depending on rarity).

You can sell a number of pre-1965 quarters for between $4 and $5 – that's at least a 10-fold profit. These feature Washington, Standing Liberty or Barber (he was an engraver). These coins in mint condition, which are hard to find, will reach nearer $300–$500.

If you have 4,000 quarters, and you find five or six of these coins among them, you'll be looking at a tidy profit by simply putting in a bit of time. And if it fails, you can take the coins back to the bank, making it a no-risk gamble.

In the UK, it's a bit different. Instead of the silver content, you would be looking for the collectibles. As Lee touched on earlier, just finding one Kew Gardens 50p in a huge withdrawal of coins could mean a 200-fold return.

We put this into plan into action and went into a big bank branch with £250 cash and asked for all 50ps, importantly that had been circulated, in return. That gave us 500 50p coins. We sifted through them and found 39 coins of interest, but sadly not the Kew Gardens Holy Grail. Of this, we unearthed a Peter Rabbit 2018 coin worth around a fiver to collectors (going by eBay sold prices and some of the coin website resources out there), along with an Athletics 2011 coin worth around £2, an NHS coin worth around £1.80 and a bunch of other coins potentially worth two or three times face value.

We returned the 461 coins we didn't need with minimum fuss, and calculated our haul to be worth somewhere between £45 and £55. This would mean an overall return of around £25 when you factor in the face value. Not bad for an hour's work.

Now for an even crazier version of this. A few years back, I bought a pile of rejected coins from a company called Fourex. This company has machines dotted around Britain used for exchanging foreign currency. When I say a pile of coins, it ended up being a bathtub full of largely rusty coins. Lee and I spent time sifting through them all, hunting out anything that looked unusual and rare.

There were many euros – we cleaned them up to make them useable again – which helped make profits. My outlay for this huge convoy of coins was £3,200. It took weeks to go through them and, in total, I made £4,000 in profit.

But, you've got to factor in time here – while on the face of it that profit looks good, in reality, it drained my time, which could have been spent doing resale elsewhere. I'll go into the importance of time versus profit in a future lesson.

ACTION POINT: Got some spare cash sitting in the bank? The next time you are in your local branch, ask them for as many 50p coins as you can get. Take them home and have a dig! Have they given you one of the rare Kew Gardens coins? The best part about this? There's no risk necessary! Win or lose, you can deposit all the coins back into your account at no loss, and have a little bit of fun in the process.

CAN OR CAR: IT ALL HAS VALUE

We had a lesson earlier about recycling and, actually, that is a core example of how everything has value. I went to the supermarket to buy 30 beers while writing this book. Afterwards, I can recycle and get money back from the aluminium. Scrap dealers will pay you for it.

An empty beer can is trash for most people. But if you see it differently, this is actual money – you can turn your can, which you wanted as it contained the drink, into cash. Whether it's a beer can, a book on buying and selling, an antique car, furniture or clothes, it doesn't change the core concept. Everything has monetary value.

There is a misconception when it comes to buying and selling that you need to deal in antiques, wooden furniture or porcelain from the Ming dynasty if you want to make serious cash. We want people to take that perspective so they overlook the opportunities we're going to find, using the tips we're going to cover as we go along.

I'm a big dude with facial hair, but if I see an old-school Barbie that I know from experience will turn a tidy profit, I'll buy it all day long. Strip away your preconceptions and don't pigeonhole yourself. Be boring, be lame: these opportunities are overlooked – you can make some serious money and guarantee to never go broke.

KEY POINTS TO RECAP

- Even boring items or those you don't think have value, will have some value. Investigate.
- Don't throw anything away without properly checking its value, even if you think it's junk.
- Think about the ratio when it comes to profit. It's often better to make 1,000 per cent profit than 0.1 per cent, even if the actual value is lower.
- Learn the value for certain items and brands as you go along. It's incredibly useful when you're at all kinds of resale events.
- Coins are a great example of value – at face value, a 50p coin is worth 50p, but not if it is an unusual one you find in your change. This is true of all manner of items.
- Don't overlook simply opportunities – junk heading to the bin can be turned into recycled cash.

LESSON 7: RESALE TRAPS TO AVOID AND TIPS FOR SUCCESS

When it comes to resale, there are a number of traps you can fall into right at the beginning and I want to help you dodge them to minimize disappointment. There are also a number of simple tips and methods to help you succeed.

There is a danger that you spread yourself too thin at the beginning. That is, you try to find an item worth a fortune and end up chasing your tail. In reality, it is all about carving out a few niche areas and concentrating on genres and items that you genuinely like. That way, you are reducing risk.

I started with video games, because I love video games. If it all went wrong, if I ever wanted to give up or life got in the way, what would be the worst that could happen? I would be left with a pile of games I liked. I can live with that.

As you grow with the resale game, you will end up spotting specialist items that you never knew about a short while ago, because your resale knowledge tree and its branches are always growing and weathering storms. It's also about taking those small wins, especially in the beginning. It's worth turning £1 into £2, £5 into £10 and building up these small profits, rather than piling into something pricey and getting in over your head.

Essentially, you'll want to have a few niche genres and items to keep picking up and learning about, while keeping your profits ticking over with bread-and-butter items that you can scoop up and sell for modest returns. How much does bread and butter cost? You'll have an idea. If a sourdough loaf goes on sale for 1p, you'll know it is a bargain.

What these bread-and-butter items are for me is seeing something for sale for £20, knowing that elsewhere it can sell for £40, £75 or even

£100. Or if it is available for £2, reselling it for £4, £7.50 or £10. You're going to need some haggling skills too. I'll help you brush up on them here. No risk, all reward.

FIND YOUR OWN 'BOOMBOX' NICHE

It's easy to think you're going to set out to find a priceless antique or speciality item that is worth tonnes of money – whether you are at a car boot sale or antiques shop – but it's harder than it sounds. One of the main reasons is that there are so many other antiques dealers and collectors who already know the true value of common names that will sell for big bucks.

What you need to do is identify 'rare' items, but not necessarily rare in terms of being scarce. Rare because people don't think they have value, when in reality, they do. A good example is vintage electronics. Many people will overlook these items at car boot sales as they may not be working and they don't have the nous or energy to get them repaired, or don't know if they are completely unsalvageable.

One of the biggest misconceptions in resale (and antiques) is the 'expert'. It just doesn't matter anymore. Experience? Sure. But accessibility of information now makes this title quite arbitrary outside of insurance policies. Sorry, Mr. Dickinson.

Sone of my biggest scores at car boot sales in recent years have been boomboxes from the 1980s and 90s. (Not because I want to play old cassette tapes or look cool in front of my friends in the mean streets of LA, London or Lancashire, hanging around basketball courts blaring out Ice Cube.) No, I picked boomboxes as I quickly established how much value they hold and sellers seem oblivious. They just want rid of their chunky old machines that probably haven't been used for decades. I have bought exactly 97 of them, all for a total price of less than £500 – or around a fiver a boom.

I have flipped them and made more than £5,000. I have held on to some of them as I believe they will continue to grow in value as the retro revival, especially for all things 1990s, continues apace and they look cool in my home.

Why did I pick boomboxes? Let's be honest, how much more appealing are mobile phones with music-streaming apps than analogue speakers in a 10lb plastic box requiring 17 D batteries (those serious, heavy duty batteries that cost a small fortune) to work?

I'm not a boombox expert by any stretch of the imagination – well, at least I wasn't when I bought my first one for a few bucks. When I bought that first one, I didn't set out to snap up so many. But if I see one at a car boot sale, I'll probably buy it if I can get it for a good price.

The fact that I am able to get such a deal on them is because I recognized that no one – or hardly anyone – seems to know the true value of these boomboxes. They are highly collectible, especially in Japan and certain urban parts of the US. If you think about it, how many retro fashion photo shoots in recent times have you seen featuring a boombox? Quite a few I would hazard a guess.

A boombox wouldn't look out of place, say, in Shoreditch or Manchester these days, with kids reviving all of the old 90s brands such as Ellesse and Kappa. With everything now going digital, physical items that you know are hand built with components and wiring are becoming more collectible. I've paid $5 for a Sony boombox that's worth $180 but most people wouldn't know that – I have carved a niche. Find yours, research it and go hunting.

I'm not saying boomboxes are the next big fad but there's enough stuff out there that you're going to recognize a niche that no one's taking advantage of – and you can swoop in and grab it like the profit-generating vulture you are becoming.

My biggest boombox score? I bought a Sharp GF-777 boombox at a random swap meet a few years ago for $7. They regularly sell online for around $1,300. Seven flipping bucks! A return of nearly 18,500 per cent.

One person I know focuses on old bicycles. He buys them, upcycles them and turns them for a profit. People are back in love with retro bikes with baskets, or certain makes such as Bianchi, Colnago or Peugeot. While out hunting, he has gathered the data and knowledge over the years to know what will turn the biggest profit. It is his wheelhouse (literally). It's all about finding your own niche that others are not taking advantage of.

You should be aiming to be constantly building – not just your bankroll – but your knowledge. You want to become an expert on your niche and know what to keep your eye out for to turn a profit. I'll mention the cameras again too here – I always now hunt for those Leica cameras and other brands I know could turn a profit, if the price is right.

When I go from one car boot sale to the next, I know a Sony boombox in yellow, for example, is always going to be worth at least £75. I know that any Japanese makes – Sanyo, Yamaha – will have a bottom price on which I base my decision. I know this bottom price because I have bought and flipped them so many times. I'm gleaning the knowledge as I go along like a resale elephant, instead of jumping from one thing to the next without rhyme or reason like a resale flea.

On the flipside, this tactic can go wrong. It is not completely foolproof, but you'll be hedging your bets by having that focus. Of the nearly one hundred boomboxes I have bought, around ten of them have had broken knobs because the set deck wasn't working properly, and to find a boombox repairman is not easy, nor is a replacement part for a specific model. No, scratch that, it's impossible.

You're not going to hit a homerun every single time – but from my boombox example, nine in ten of my purchases have resulted in profit, a pretty fine return. If you hedge your bets where you're not 100 per cent sure of the value, but the price is so low, one way or another you'll win in the end.

A NIFTY BARCODE TRICK FOR YOUR BREAD-AND-BUTTER ITEMS

While many use barcode-scanning apps in their own homes (see Lesson 1, page 55), they are great when you're out and about too. They can help you build up your bread-and-butter returns, which should complement your niche items.

You can scan media at car boot sales and even charity shops for quick wins. You will need a smartphone and internet connection for this. You might find that a DVD being sold for 50p is worth £5 on the app – a ten-fold profit.

Now you may think that is a bit of a nasty move to pull on a charity shop or the seller at a car boot sale. But it isn't. These are items that have been handed in to a charity shop or a person no longer wants in their home. You're paying what they're asking for it – essentially, everyone's a winner. Take advantage. Books can be gold dust using this trick, especially relatively up-to-date academic ones.

Using the barcode trick is a surefire way to give your coffers a boost. Find your own multimedia niche, whether it is parenting books, *Marvel* DVDs or PS3 games. As you grow, you'll know with a quick eye exactly what genres and specific films will be worth snapping up this way to sell on quickly for profit.

This is a core concept – take advantage of all the money-making opportunities out there, even if it does feel a little weird to be wandering around a charity shop scanning items.

SMALL WIN VERSUS BIG HIDDEN HOMERUN

Many towns and cities have seen a rise in charity shops and I would go and hit a load at the same time to maximize time and transport costs. You want to focus on a quantity of small wins rather than trying to find a big, hidden homerun. You want to turn a profit.

If you're starting out, your mindset should be: I need to turn a profit as quickly as possible, I don't need to overthink it and I need to get on the scoreboard. Basically, you need to learn to walk before you run.

You don't need to go too crazy – it's about finding that perfect balance between mitigating your risk, lowering your costs, turning a quick profit and collecting that money to reinvest into yourself and into buying more items, especially while you discover your niche. Get on base before trying for a homerun.

ACTION POINT: Get scanning – find the biggest book in your local charity shop and give it a scan using one of our recommended book-scanning apps (see page 55). What is the price that shows up? If it's more than the charity shop's asking price, do a quick flip. Not every giant book is worth a fortune but more than likely, academic and large, colourful coffee-table books will have more value than smaller print and paperback books. It's an easy way to get started on quick-flip opportunities in charity shops.

THE ART OF THE HAGGLE – STOP BEING SO BRITISH!

A key skill that many Britons struggle with is the art of the haggle. Have no shame. You're in it to make profits. Americans are brash and just go for it. But you Brits? Well, you're just too damn polite! More often than not, people want to get rid of their stuff. That is fundamentally what they are there for. Your aim? Get it for a better price than they want for it.

If you don't ask, you won't get. The core principle to remember is that nobody will bite your head off. The worst thing they can say? 'No', then you walk away. More often than not, that walking away will be the catalyst to be called back and a deal will follow.

Now, many great folks are scared when it comes to this. It's all about saving as much money as possible, to make chunkier profits. Just think about it: 99.9 per cent of the time, it is unlikely you will ever see the person you are haggling with ever again. If you are likely to see them again during your resale ventures – an antiques dealer, say, rather than someone at a car boot sale – make sure you don't completely lowball them. I'll explain why in the lesson about contact building and marketing (see page 155).

All people care about is your money and all you should care about is making money. When you find something that you like and you encounter the seller, this is when you have your poker game. The idea is simple: getting whatever you want for as cheaply as possible.

Now, that doesn't necessarily mean offering a quid for an item that could be worth £100. It's about finding that reasonable price point – you're reading someone to see what their happy spot is. I like to call it their H-Spot.

There are a couple of ways you can do this and safety nets you can use to prevent a deal going bad. For example, you find something you know is worth an easy £100 – and that's what they're selling it for. How do you drive them down as low as possible?

If they're firm on the price and they won't take any less than £100, you can still ask the questions and see where you end up. Usually, as a rule of thumb, I won't offer below half of their original asking price. So if they want £100 for it, my starting point will be £50.

Remember, you're going to want to make a tidy profit on the item you're buying. This is the safety net to seal the deal. The reason they're there is to make as much money as possible, but crucially also to take home as few items as they can.

Going back to the deal, let's just go with the expectation you want to spend no more than £75 on this item. My advice to you is to offer £50. They're probably going to say no and they'll usually offer it for somewhere around £80 to £90. But now what you're establishing is the 50/50 game. You always want to meet back in the middle. So if you say £50 and they say £90, the follow-up answer is, 'I'm willing to meet you in the middle and I'll do £70'.

This makes you look like the good guy who's willing to negotiate and be reasonable – aim for the middle. Your ridiculous original offer becomes more respectable and, in turn, the seller will usually consider it more seriously. He may throw out a counter-offer, maybe £80, but you say £75, stick out a hand and more often than not, this tactic works.

The seller feels good to have haggled, you'll feel good to have haggled – and won.

And unless there's someone standing next to you who's interested in buying that same item, time is on your side. You have a good sixty-second window to change your mind although, if you have shaken on it, it would be very poor form. They can't change their mind really, but as a buyer, you can before you hand them the money.

If you are struggling to meet a price point you feel comfortable with, say you'll think about it and walk away, as I previously mentioned. I'm telling you now 75 per cent of the time they will stop you and accept the £75 before you walk away completely because they're losing an easy sell right there and then. The fear may set in that they won't get that good an offer for the rest of the day, month or year.

If they don't stop you, you could come right back around and do the deal anyway, but the key concept here is not about what other people think about you or what the seller thinks about you. It's just about how much money can you save to turn a greater profit.

The core concept with haggling is half – always half, half, half, in one direction or another, to try to save as much money as possible.

It's also worth looking at an item and verifying on eBay or elsewhere your price decision. This can focus your negotiation tactics. Be reasonable, be respectable, loosen up and have a little fun with it because that's the whole point of the game. And usually, it'll work out in your favour one way or another.

FINDING THE RIGHT BALANCE OF PERSONALITY

It's worth noting here that you want to find the right balance of personality when you're haggling. You want to come across as a good person, not someone taking advantage.

But in that same breath, you don't want to act too excited, showing a weakness or letting them know that you really want a certain item and you'll part with whatever it takes to get it. Don't come across as a swindler but don't be overconfident and look like a sucker. Find that sweet spot between swindler and sucker for the best results.

Some choose what I call the *Pawn Stars* strategy of haggling where you always find a fault with any item, whether electronics, clothes or anything else. You try to convince the seller that you're the only person willing to pay this amount for it – you're the only game in town. You've got to do a deal with me or you're never going to be able to sell it. This is a more brash approach and it only works if you are super-confident and you're not too bothered about what people think of you.

DON'T BE AFRAID TO WALK AWAY

I'll say it again – don't be afraid to walk away. You might find the same item at the next stall, shop or dealer away. Don't fall for FOMO (fear of missing out). It happens.

Whatever deal you may have missed, there is another one right around the corner. I was looking at an awesome set of Tommy Hilfiger luggage at a car boot sale recently. The gentleman wanted $30 for it. I offered $20 but he wouldn't take less than $25. I didn't want to pay more. After much contemplation, I decided to walk. Little did I know, 50 feet away someone was selling the same exact luggage! The final selling price? $10!

On this note, don't become emotionally attached to an item you're looking to buy or have bought. Look at it as profit potential – an item you're going to have for a very short space of time that will be sold on quickly. You'll have to accept that, sometimes, this means walking away and not buying an item you had your heart set on, because you couldn't get it for the right price.

BUY ITEMS THAT YOU LOVE

When starting out, one of the best ways to minimize risk is to focus on items and genres that you genuinely like or love. Are you a sports fan? Focus on memorabilia and kits. Do you love fashion? Focus on finding good-quality labels you'll slowly build up knowledge on. Whatever your passions are, focus on that first.

There are a couple of reasons why I recommend this approach and it will become even clearer in later lessons. Firstly, if you don't manage to sell the item or items you've bought, at least you'll be left with something you like, love or care about, rather than some random knick-knack.

Secondly, at the beginning, if it is an area of life you are interested in, you're more likely to put your heart and soul into learning about the items, and the market. My passion at the start was arcade gaming machines. I immersed myself in that world, gleaned knowledge along the way.

As time has gone on, I've added to this area of niche – that's where your own personal boombox niche will come into play. As you grow and learn about resale, you'll start falling down a few rabbit holes, finding that you become an expert as you go along.

YOU CAN'T KNOW THE VALUE OF EVERYTHING

When it comes to resale, there is a danger of spreading yourself too thin – you try to become a walking encyclopedia on a million-and-one items, rather than narrowing your focus. It's important to remember that you'll never be an expert in everything – and the faster you learn that, the better. It is better to concentrate on a handful of genres at the start of your resale journey.

Once you have mastered them, you can bring other items into your arsenal and build up a portfolio of items you have become an 'expert' in. The resale game is a difficult beast to tame, but once you nail those core items, you will know – and then, you can start to think about expanding.

The game has changed. The world is too fluid and prices can be dictated by a single celebrity tweet, rather than a price guide or traditional buy and hold methods. Patterns can be found in the world of resale, but some things change in value for no good reason.

When YouTube star Logan Paul started buying and opening first edition Pokémon packs on his channel to unearth the rarest cards he could find, the interest inflated card values exponentially – as much as ten times the value from the previous year. It made millennials pine for their youth and go crazy for Pokémon all over again.

THE RESALE TREE

We want you to imagine your resale journey like a family tree. But instead of family members, we want your branches to represent all the core areas you're interested in and see where they take you. For example, one branch of my tree starts with video games because that's where my resale career began. Off this branch comes audio, then off that other speciality niches such as boomboxes and radio tubes.

As you grow in expertise and add new niche areas to your searches, this tree should grow from a puny little sapling to a great big mighty oak as your tree of knowledge grows and spreads.

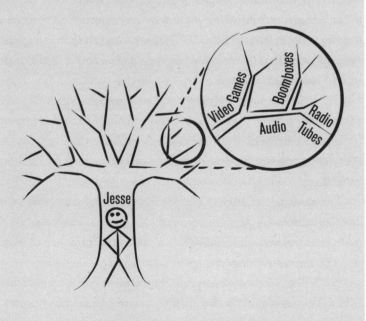

ACTION POINT: Copy this tree to add your own name and start filling in your resale niches on the branches.

THE DANGER OF PIGEONHOLING YOURSELF

On the flipside of the above, one of the most important secrets to being good at making profits is to avoid pigeonholing yourself or boxing yourself into just one specific item. Don't focus on just one thing: try to understand there is a limited opportunity to take advantage of a particular object – whether you're buying or selling – and milk it for everything it's got until you can move on.

Some items could be short term and others longer term, but the idea is you're not going to put all your eggs into one basket. From a personal finance perspective, we're always told the importance of diversifying – and it is similar in the resale game. You want to be ahead of the curve when an opportunity dries up.

FINDING A DIAMOND IN A PILE OF RUBIES

It's best not to think about finding a diamond in the rough, but rather finding a diamond in a pile of rubies. This is about identifying items that experts have that aren't part of their expertise. I see examples of this all the time.

While I was in Las Vegas, I went to a charity clothing shop that had been donated a box of a hundred beauty products. They were sitting in a cardboard box on the floor with a marker labelled '99 cents each'. I offered to buy the whole box for $50, which they gladly accepted. The manager was delighted because they were a burden for her – they took up space that could be used for the clothing they so easily sold.

Inside the box were sealed Kerastase products, which I bulk sold to an online beauty supply company for $10.38...each. How they got to that specific price is anyone's guess, but I took advantage. I repeat: I am a man with a beard, backwards cap and little knowledge of beauty products but I saw what was inside, quickly searched the products online and knew it was a steal.

The shop was too focused on vintage clothing. They didn't necessarily know the true value of that box – it was an opportunity to swoop in. You never know what kind of deals you can find this way and I do it all the time.

For example, I might find a person just selling tools at a car boot sale, but they might have some other miscellaneous stuff from their house that they're just trying to offload on their stall. They have no idea about it, but I do.

Or I might come across someone selling just books, but they have a few other bits and pieces that don't fall into that category. So they are willing to offload them for next to nothing as they have no interest in them. They just want them gone.

RINSE AND REPEAT

In a later lesson, I will reveal all about how I started with arcade machines, going from one video game to 109 arcade units. I could have stopped halfway through and been happy, but I decided to keep on going. There's no wrong answer here as to when to stop. The core message is to reinvest and sell, rinse, repeat and go on and on as far as you can, if you want to.

People start to get into trouble if, once they sell an item, they take that money and use it for something else that isn't related to buying and selling, whether it's going out with friends, shopping, bills or anything else. You need to set aside this money to reinvest in your company, your business; and your other money, wherever it may come from, you can use for any other expenses you may have.

Naturally, the opportunity to reinvest will eventually peter out. That is, it's unlikely that you can take it any further. In terms of my arcade selling, I stopped at 109 machines because I became fed up with collecting all the quarters from the various locations, but also I wanted some of the money as a down payment on my first home.

Did I set out to do that? No. But I knew it was time to cash in and use the money elsewhere. However, some of it I did set aside to reinvest again. This is where having a segregated pot of cash will prove hugely useful.

START SMALL – IT'LL HELP YOU LEARN

We want to make your journey into resale as minimal a risk as possible. That is, we want you to build that free pot of cash and, when it comes to the trade up, start small. That way, you're not overexposing yourself by buying pricey items you might get burned on. Get those small wins under your belt and keep trying to trade up.

Also, don't think in terms of targets – for example, turning this £10 item and trading up and trading up to make £100,000. There will be hiccups along the way. Don't overthink it. Use the core concepts from *Never Go Broke* and go slow and steady.

Remember, this isn't a get-rich-quick book. It is a never-go-broke, make-money-on-the-side book, with the potential to get rich (later...).

KEY POINTS TO RECAP

- Find some niche items and genres and learn about them as you go along.
- Use your barcode-scanning app to bag those all-important bread-and-butter items.
- Remember to haggle. Do it fairly, and do it right.
- Abandon FOMO – walk away if you don't get the price you want when buying an item.
- Focus on items and genres you are interested in, at least at the start.
- Small wins are important to keep building up your pot of cash.
- You can't know the value of everything. Focus on a few items and keep building your repertoire.
- Don't pigeonhole yourself entirely – that is, don't box yourself into just one item.
- Sometimes, the best item can be where you're not expecting to find it. Keep your eyes open at all times.
- Keep your resale pot separate from life. Don't be tempted to dip into it, at least not in the beginning.

LESSON 8: HOW TO VALUE YOUR PRECIOUS TIME

Time is money. The more time you faff around trying to source and sell items, the lower your hourly, weekly, monthly – and ultimately your annual – wage from this becomes. You need to be aware about how much time you put into resale and make decisions as to whether certain items are worth your time.

There are so many easy, quick wins out there – usually for small gains – but people fall into the trap of doing the opposite. We want to hammer home the idea that the quicker you can get items and move them on, the more time you'll have to repeat the process and swell your coffers.

That will mean more money coming in and, ultimately, a bigger pot of resale cash. The feeling of momentum is thrilling. You don't want to be stuck in quicksand when it comes to resale.

TIME *REALLY* IS MONEY

Let me start off by giving you a real flavour of what I'm talking about. I was doing a house clearance and came across a microphone, all in pieces. It needed some work to fix it up, which I'll explain in a later lesson.

The microphone was an RCA 44-BX model. I quickly realized it was worth around $3,000, give or take, and I had bagged it as part of a $2,000 haul, which included loads of other items. Your gut reaction might be to sell it online. That's where the quickest sale will be with the largest audience to maximize profits. But, in reality, it's probably not. Let me explain.

There's a website that is essentially a marketplace for vintage music equipment. The microphone would sell for around $2,500–$3,000 on this site, which would take a 12 per cent cut. Depending on the selling price, the cut would be anywhere between $250 and $350. I have to factor that into my profit margin. Now I'm dealing with a net profit of $2,200 to $2,700, but I also have to factor in the time it takes to make my listing and ship it, and the delivery costs involved. Delivery costs would need to cover a signature on arrival and insurance in case it is damaged or lost in transit, making it quite expensive given its size.

If it ends up selling to someone thousands of miles away, I'm looking at $100 of transport costs, so my net profit is down to $2,100 to $2,600. I'm also likely to be dealing with someone who I've never met, for thousands of pounds. Potential scammers are always around, especially on the internet, circling around like the keyboard sharks they are.

My other selling option is that I have a contact who knows a contact (I'll explain how to build up a contact book in the next lesson). He wants to buy it right away, but for $1,600. Whoa, hold on there Jesse, you're telling me you'd sell it for less than it's worth?

What it's worth is what someone is willing to pay for it. Yes, I may have bagged $2,700 online, but this guy is here and ready to buy, today. No shipping costs. No listing time. No scam. Cash, in my hand, ready to flow into the next resale item. In the end, we haggled and he paid $1,900 for it.

On paper, comparatively, I'm losing somewhere around $300–$500 on the sale – although I'm still majorly up on the outlay of it. It's about finding the sweet spot which is, in essence, the time I'm saving and the risk I'm avoiding. I can take this money now – cash in hand – and move on to my next thing, or I could spend the time and try to milk a few hundred dollars extra.

What is my time worth? It's important for people to quantify.

If you don't really understand what your time is worth, then you will prevent yourself from continuously making profits. It's not always necessarily about making the most amount of profit you can on an item – it's more about what's the best profit you can make in as little time as possible.

If you spent two days, that's 16 hours, listing an item to eke out an extra £200, you're starting to talk about less than the magic £10 an hour, which could bring you down to minimum wage or below. You have to ask yourself: is that worth it? Or can I spend my time, which could be paying me £25 to £35 an hour, better than trying to milk out this last couple of hundred pounds.

It's so important to think about your time as a monetary figure, rather than thinking you are losing out on a couple of hundred pounds. It's easier for you to make a decision that way. And understand, again, your own personal value, not just the value in the item you're trying to sell.

This becomes more important as time goes on – you'll need to factor any part-time or full-time job you have into the equation as well.

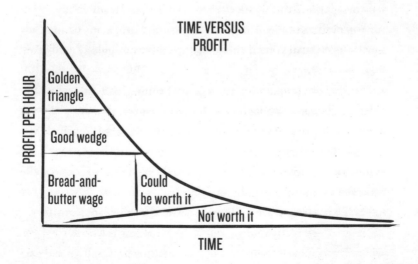

REBATE VERSUS PROFIT

Just because something is 'worth' a certain amount, doesn't mean you can sell it for that worth. It is only worth what a buyer is willing to pay, and that can mean taking the occasional hit. The important thing is not to hold on to something for too long and be adamant you're only selling it for a certain price – you will occasionally need to let go.

Whether you look it up online or someone tells you an item's value, rebate versus profit is about maximizing your potential profit on any given item. That doesn't change. The idea is about perspective – it's easy to sell something for £1 if it cost you £1. Ideally, it'd be more than this, but that won't always be the case.

Let's say you bought something at retail price, and now you're looking to sell it on – this happens quite a bit, especially with electronics.

Some people get so adamant about selling it on their own via eBay, that they stray away from the whole point of this. If you hold on to everything to try to find the maximum potential profit, you'll never sell anything and this whole endeavour will become pointless.

You need to look at it in terms of turning a profit, so you may feel a little uncertain if you make less than what you originally paid for it. I like to treat that as getting a rebate. If I bought something for £100 and used it for a few months for a certain purpose, then sold it for £90, at least I got good use out of it before I sold it on. I've received most of my money back. It's more of a mindset than an applied principle.

The idea is that you take an item, sell it as quickly as possible for as much as possible and then move on to the next thing. Occasionally it's a rebate instead of a profit, but the idea is that there's always going to be cash in your pocket and you're ready for the next opportunity.

WHY ITEMS NEED AN EXPIRY DATE

How do you proactively take a loss and happily walk away with your tail between your legs? I call it being happily embarrassed.

My success rate on items is 90 per cent or more. That's because I've found my own blueprint and learned as I've gone along. It's not always been at that level. When you start out your success rate will probably be 40–60 per cent. That'll eventually head higher because you'll start knowing your own market, and we're giving you a head start with this book.

When is the breaking point, when you have to let go of an item and try to recover as much of your investment back as you can? You will have failures and some items just won't work out, but please do not fret. You may even accidentally break something – a repair that you can't fix.

How do you get rid of that item? What you need to do is establish a sense of inventory control and, at some point say, 'I need to put this in the clearance section'.

Think about it in terms of a department store. You can trace the timeline of a jumper from when it first comes out in front of the store at full retail price, brand new, in stock. Then the next season comes in and it gets pushed somewhere in the middle. There'll be an offer: buy two for £35, something like that.

Three to six months down the line, whatever's left over is pushed to the back to the clearance section. That's when they get discounted. It's best to keep a department store mindset like this. Have that methodology in mind in your day-to-day buying and selling, whether you're at a car boot sale, have an eBay business or your own retail shop.

At the car boot sale, this could be the first two hours at the front of your stall, second two hours in the middle, and third it's simply got to go. It does not matter what the item is, establish a timeline. For me, most of the items I buy and sell I give a six-month expiry date. What is yours? It could be six months, a year, just make sure you have it in mind.

I break it down into thirds. For the first two months, the price is 80–100 per cent of my intended target. For the next two months, I would accept 40–70 per cent. For the last two months I'd take 0–40 per cent. It doesn't matter what the prices are or what the item is. You're just putting it in the formula.

This will be essential so you don't end up marrying an item or becoming a bag holder. It could be handy to have an inventory list written down somewhere, with timeframes and target values in mind. You have an expiry date on milk. If you didn't, it would just sit in your fridge curdling.

ACTION POINT: Create your own personal 'record book', listing items with expiry dates and target prices. Start documenting how fast you sell items. What is the quickest time? Try to beat it.

EXPIRY DATE

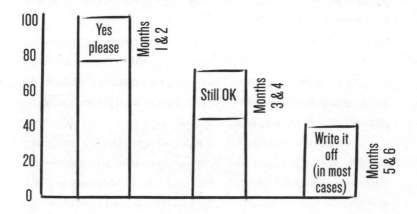

BULK BUYING CAN SOMETIMES PAY OFF (BIG TIME)

On the whole, bulk buying is more of a professional resale gig – that is, it's not an ideal stomping ground for beginners. You don't want to be left with a pile of items you cannot shift because you took on more than you could chew. I have a great story about this in a later lesson where someone I met bought a pile of fad items. Sadly the fad went as quickly as it came. Bulk buying items you think are on trend is not a good idea – however, bulk buying items that have a consistent value can reap rewards.

At one swap meet, I bought a seller's entire collection of 'vintage' clothes. Let me explain the process of why I did this and the lesson you can take from it. The seller had approximately 300 pieces for sale. Of these, I was very interested in about 100 items, semi-interested in about 100 items, and the other 100 had value, but weren't exactly what I was after.

With selling prices of $3–$10, I was looking at a total cost of $2,000–$3,000 if bought individually. I knew that I could double my money on the full cost of the 100 items I was interested in, so my approach was simple – offer him $1,000 for the entire lot.

As a seller at a car boot sale, someone offering you $1,000 as opposed to $5–$10 per item sounds incredibly enticing. But from the buyer's perspective, this is a 66 per cent discount. Car boot sales are an ideal place to make such offers as people don't want to go home with items. He accepted with little hesitation or haggling.

Why exactly did I pay 'full price' for the items I wanted though? Because the other 200 pieces I knew could easily hedge my 'gamble' and would pay for the entire lot. I knew I could sell them for at least $1,000 total, making the pieces I actually wanted nearly, if not completely, 100 per cent free.

Think of bulk buying as hedging your bets. 'Throw-ins', although they may seem of little importance, can certainly add up over time to help lower your risk in purchases. This is quite an advanced level, however – I'd only go down this route when you are entirely comfortable, have the money to make this kind of deal, have future buyers in mind and are able to calculate the profit potential on items quickly. It can save a whole heap of time.

When a new games system or electronics comes out, or I find an item that is on a limited-time sale and I know will go back up in price, I usually buy two or three of them to cover 50 per cent or 100 per cent of the cost of my item. (And only two or three: I'm talking to you, toilet paper and PlayStation 5 hoarders.)

Take advantage as you see fit. Worse case scenario: you can always return it if it doesn't work out. Take advantage within the rules, but don't be greedy or cheat the system.

IT DOESN'T NEED TO BE A FULL-TIME OR EVEN PART-TIME JOB

Find ways to lower your risk. If I eat a new type of food for dinner, I'll always have my favourite dessert on hand in case things go wrong. I'm taking the risk by trying something new I may never knew I loved, but I'm not risking total misery if my culinary gamble turns out to be a surprise mushroom (yuck) or olive (double yuck).

In my resale life, I have done so many different things. Some gigs have felt like a full-time, whole day of hard graft – like selling in my parents' antiques shop or clearing out entire homes. Others I have treated as part-time, fun activities, like going to car boot sales looking to make my set daily 'wage', which could be anything from £50 to £500.

I used to do house clearances and take home 50 per cent of the profit I made on items I found. All I had to do was market and organize it and I could make £3,000 in a weekend. Typically, it would take me roughly 10 hours to clear a home. That brings my hourly wage to £300 per hour. But then it could take me another 10 or 20 hours on average to sort through which item belonged in which resale tier, clean them up and market them. At the quicker end of the scale, that would mean £150 per hour. At the slower end, £100 an hour.

The point I'm trying to make here once again is that you do have to establish how much your time is worth – an hourly wage.

ACTION POINT: What is your time worth? Have a think about it and crunch some figures. Take all of your income for the week: your normal wage if you are employed, your total from your week of sales, and any other income you may have made. Divide the total by 40, and that is your hourly life wage. The number doesn't matter, it's more about adding value to your life and accomplishments. Big or small, be proud of what you've done.

TAKE THESE TIPS AS FAR AS YOU WANT, THERE IS NO MINIMUM REQUIREMENT...

It's up to you to decide. Making small profits might not be very appealing. However, if you do it passively and recognize the potential profit while you're doing something else, it can be extremely rewarding. For instance, taking out the trash and bringing something back with you as you were there already feels great. You're making profit by simply going about your day-to-day life.

This can be fun and you can learn along the way. It is quite simple to fit some of this into the hobby category. You're not going out of your way or ruining a daily structure. You can find massive scores by doing very little and I adore resale for this. My message is that it doesn't need to get in the way of anything you are doing right now. It can be passive if you want to do it that way.

Let me give another example. My mum is not really into resale. But being around my dad and I, if she goes into a thrift store to look for something she needs, she will also look at the collectibles, the vinyl. She might just spot an item for a few quid she knows will make a profit as she knows what to look out for – she has it in her resale muscle memory.

She doesn't spend any extra time or effort hunting down items, she roughly knows what it is worth and whether it is a good idea to snap it up. She's not doing this full time or even part time. She just happens to be in the area.

This is a great example as to why this book can be applicable to everybody's life. They can deny they are in it at all, while making money without really trying. It's a magical thing. Get rich(ish) quick(ish). My favourite dessert? Free. My actual favourite dessert? Hot fudge brownie sundae.

THE PAPERCLIP TALE

I love trading. It's how I started my resale life. It's a beautiful art form. One of my favourite stories tells of how someone traded up from a paperclip to a house. It's a wonderful example of how it all works, showing trade can be as vital as a sale.

If you're not familiar with the story, essentially a man from Canada managed to turn a single red paperclip into a house in a series of 14 online trade ups. They included swapping an afternoon with Alice Cooper and even a role in a movie. This garnered plenty of publicity and happened in 2005, at the dawn of people going 'viral' on the internet.

The house, in Kipling, Saskatchewan, was in part a huge publicity stunt. The economic development officer at the time proposed to the council that they should make that trade happen. Why? Well it's a good draw for some tourism to the town – they even put up the world's biggest paperclip on the side of it. The home was said to be worth $45,000–$50,000.

The chances of you replicating this story are slimmer than slim, unless you manage to get a huge bout of publicity behind you, but there are no doubts numerous people have tried to do it. The red paperclip story is sexy, sure, but don't think of the trading path as linear, just hope for movement in the right general direction (even if it's forward, but also a bit left).

This is an extreme example and a good pub story. It fires up the imagination. I do use trading up in my own resale life to save time. I have traded items, sometimes to go from A, to B, to C, to D and then stop, or sometimes from A, to B, to C, to D and all the way to J or K.

Trading instead of selling can sometimes be a worthwhile avenue to explore. Just manage your expectations. Don't expect to trade a paperclip for a home – especially given the average UK house price is beyond the £200,000 mark

THE CORE CONCEPT: FIND YOUR PAPERCLIP

The lesson here is the simple concept of reinvesting in your business. Trading can lead you from A to B, C, D, C, B, K, then to Z – one step backwards to go two steps forwards. You can call it a business, you can call it reinvesting in yourself or just reinvesting in your items. The idea is, that if you take a smaller item – a low-cost one – and sell it or trade it, you can use that to buy or trade to something bigger and better.

You can then rinse and repeat. The idea is, eventually, as you buy low and sell high, your profits are going to slowly increase. I emphasize slowly here. Don't think you're going to make bumper profits all the time or straight away. The core concept, whether you trade it or sell it, is that you're going to be making a profit to reinvest and continually grow.

Find your own paperclip. To start with, I'd pick a genre of something you're interested in and like, as I've previously pointed out. If you buy and sell a bunch of stuff and it fails, or you give up because life happens, at least you'll be left with things you like. For me, it was video games.

ACTION POINT: Find a collection of media you have – whether it's books, movies, video games or CDs. Sort through that collection and make a pile of items that you personally value as £0 – that is, if you sold them, donated them or trashed them, you would not miss them. Now, go to a friend, neighbour or family member, and see what they are willing to trade for an item. Whether the item they offer in exchange is higher, lower or equal in value, if it is something you actually enjoy, you will always come out ahead as it will be worth more than the item you originally valued as worthless.

WHAT TO LEARN FROM MY ARCADE TRADE

I promised to tell you about how I started and first learned everything has value. This story also highlights one of my earlier points: a good starting point for buying and selling is focusing on an area you love. A cautionary tip here, though: don't get blindsided by the love of an item or form too much of an attachment.

I started with one video game. Super Mario Bros 3, bought secondhand for a few bucks for the original Nintendo Entertainment System (which was fantastic, by the way, back when playing a console was an escape from reality – these days games are largely made to be hyper-realistic).

I learned as I went along in those early years. Of course I didn't know everything about collecting. How could I? I was young and the internet wasn't so easily available as the reference tool it is today. But as you go along, you learn the nuances of certain items, along with tips and tricks.

I bought Super Mario Bros 3 because I liked it. It ended up being my first paperclip. I sold it for around $14 because it had started to become harder to get hold of – remember, again, this was largely pre-internet days. I took that money and bought three more games.

I turned a small profit and turned that into six games. I sold and traded those into twelve games and, before long, I had traded them for a Nintendo system with nine games. This became three systems, then nine. I then traded them all for my first standalone arcade machine, Space Invaders, which cost $200.

Arcade machines are a different beast to consoles. Once again, I knew nothing, but thought it would be cool to own one and I was willing to learn. I saw the money-making potential, not just the fun. I once again managed to reinvest the profits from this machine into three machines, then nine, then twelve. Before long, I had arcade machines in different locations across my hometown, all making me a profit.

I'd made a massive profit from that one original video game. Was that my goal? Counting quarters, visiting four different locations – restaurants, fairgrounds and laundromats in Southern California – to empty the machines and collect the cash? No. But opening my mind to the idea that it could be bigger set me on the path of success.

My tree is easy to replicate. It doesn't have to be video games – whether it is cameras or vintage clothes, the principle is still the same. I was reinvesting the money. From that very first Super Mario Bros 3 game, I didn't put any more money in to my business. I was just trading and selling, trading, selling and reinvesting. The concept is that you can turn a small investment into something massive. One

Nintendo game to a fully fledged arcade business which was generating a monthly income.

I no longer have any arcade machines. I sold my entire business for around $15,000. I went from $3 to $15,000. I'll reiterate. It took three years to do this and it really was fun. However, I don't want to oversimplify it – there was hard work involved. But it wasn't complicated moving from A to Z and reinvesting into myself and my business. For me, it wasn't a business idea. I just wanted a load of video games to play and have fun. When I got bored, I traded up and resold.

Your goal may be to build a business or maybe it's just trying to enjoy yourself and have fun with things, and reinvest. It can be a great way to make a little bit more money. That's how many people treat it out there now. Instead of joining their local darts team or football league, they're getting into the resale game as a hobby. Some then find they're very good at it and go deeper and deeper.

DON'T MARRY AN ITEM

In my entire buying and selling career, I have never married an item and I'm always willing to put in a little elbow grease and time if it's going to result in a profit. Going back to the arcade story – I knew through my contacts what people were after in certain locations. I made my probability of success a lot higher, based on interest in that particular title. I was also trading one good working machine for a few that weren't in such great condition when I got them. It involved me putting in some work repairing and cleaning them after watching a whole load of tutorial videos.

I learned about the machines as I went along – how to replace a capacitor or a coin mechanism, for example. But I never went too far. If there weren't easy instructions on how to repair it, I wouldn't get the machine. Sometimes you can become too ambitious, and I have learned this lesson in the past – especially with cars, thinking I could fix something when I actually had no idea.

I had a romantic vision of fixing this Volkswagen campervan. What started out as a vehicle bargain turned into a headache so I had to pivot. I had to figure out what part was the most valuable and strip it out to maintain my hourly wage. Van surgery isn't as fun as buying video games, believe me.

You might lose some profit margin, but you can still make things happen, even if it isn't what you'd planned. Instead of me finding out how to replace the engine on a VW campervan and sell it whole, I realized I needed to figure out how to remove the engine and the other key components to sell them individually. I had to work out where the value was and cash it in.

I didn't marry that bus. I stripped it apart to keep making money and reinvesting, making sure that particular resale job didn't completely zap my time.

I am not 100 per cent perfect in the resale world, and I still take the occasional loss to this day. So, don't beat yourself up if a resale opportunity doesn't work out exactly how you'd hoped…it happens.

PROGRESS ORGANICALLY

When you're trading up, don't get caught up thinking about the end game. If you don't get a house, it's not a failure! Think instead how you can make your existing contacts, products and efforts marry together to take this as far as it can naturally go, then move on to the next opportunity. That's a better focus.

If you can manage to create a direct path between starting with this and ending with that, by all means go for it. But remember to factor in both money and time. Sometimes it's okay to stop at a certain point and move on to the next thing if you come across a different opportunity, because opportunities will arise that have no connection to your current path whatsoever.

I wasn't planning on stopping at 109 arcade machines in three locations, but I was building contacts, someone made me an offer and I found I was ready for a new challenge. I wasn't married to those arcade machines.

When I bought the first Nintendo game, my goal was never to use arcade money to put towards buying a house. How could it have been? But I sold the machines because the opportunity presented itself and it was an excellent time to buy a house, thanks to a lull in the housing market.

Don't set yourself strict goals – let things progress organically. I repeat: don't set yourself an unrealistic end goal. You do not need to be paperclip dude.

DON'T GET THREE TRANSACTIONS BEHIND

Try to to keep things fluid – if another brand new opportunity comes up, you don't want to be stuck with a build-up of a business you're trying to get out of or trade up. You'll want to avoid the time zap. Fluidity will allow you to grasp a bigger and better opportunity if one appears.

I'm a big proponent of flexibility in the resale game. I can move on quickly – from video games, to radio tubes, to vintage cameras, travelling to a brand new country or in the US, vintage clothes, whatever it may be.

I'm not stuck three transactions behind, still trying to offload my old video games before I can reinvest – I stay nimble and fluid. I'll touch more on inventory control in the next lesson.

THE SOCIAL MEDIA BLOCK

One of the biggest pitfalls in the modern world is the P-word: procrastination. For that reason, although I use the internet for resale, it is not my number one choice. I don't spend all my time checking prices, taking photographs, writing listings and going down a Wikipedia rabbit hole on a random topic, and then wonder where that last hour went.

One of the main pitfalls when it comes to the internet, and selling on social media particularly, is not describing items correctly or being controversial on the platform. People won't really like you and you won't do well.

People also get themselves caught up in this web that I like to call 'social media block'. It's this idea that you've got to look good so you put on a big show on your Instagram, with filters, gifs and stickers and all of that irritating stuff that can put the average buyer off. I can't say this enough: what you're doing is wasting valuable selling time.

My wife Nicole and I have a vintage clothing business. There's a shop in the US and in the UK. She largely runs it and her social media presence is next to none. Is that on purpose? Well, no. The reason why is this: we sell clothes so fast we don't need to waste time on our image, like setting up photoshoots with people. The work required to do that is huge – for little reward when it comes to resale.

It might make you feel good, but the reason why I tell the story about Nicole is not because I want everyone to know how awesome she is (and she might be reading this book) but to establish this: the aim is to identify a need, which should always come first before the marketing hoopla. You have to present the stuff that is establishing your customer base and get people coming back for more, knowing you are go-to for a certain item. You don't need to focus on social media before trying to convince people your stuff is good.

If your items are good, your customers will already be coming to you. If your prices are low, your customers will come. If you have something people are after, they will come – you shouldn't need to oversell something if it's already selling on its own.

It's far better to have an item that sells quickly because you've identified the need, it's good quality, you've built the customer base and it's good value, rather than spend precious time marketing one item with a photoshoot and all of the effort that goes with it.

All of this leads me nicely on to building contacts and going that next step when it comes to marketing. Promoting and marketing your business is important, don't get us wrong. But fancy social media posts shouldn't be your primary goal...they should be secondary. Don't get caught up in the hoopla.

KEY POINTS TO RECAP

- Value your time: work out, as best you can, an hourly wage when you buy an item and resell it. This will become easier as your resale life grows.
- Remember that 'rebate versus profit' mentality. Sometimes you'll have to throw your hands up and accept that you can't make a profit on everything.
- Bulk buying is largely for when you become more experienced, but it can help save time in the long run.
- You can easily build resale into your everyday life – look for those wins that are literally built into your day without having to go out of your way.
- Trading items can sometimes save time, just don't expect to be red paperclip dude.
- Don't set yourself unrealistic goals and remember that it can take work trading up, like my arcade game experience.
- Never marry an item – prepare to change your plans and let go.
- Be fluid to avoid the dreaded time zap.
- The internet can be the ultimate time waster – use it wisely.

LESSON 9: CONTACTS AND MARKETING ARE KEY

One of my core strengths is using my contacts and keeping a useful record of all the people I buy and sell from. You'll never know when you might need them again. I do this with everyone, from specialist dealers to charity shop workers. The bigger your contact book, the quicker it can be to get items appraised and sold so you can move on to the next thing.

As you grow and evolve in resale, much of the time you'll already have in mind the person you're going to sell to as you're buying an item – and they are just a phone call or message away. Plenty of times I've bought an item, made that phone call and within seconds I've sold it – flipped a profit just like that. It's so much easier than going through the rigmarole of hunting down a buyer from nowhere. It becomes easier as time goes on and your contact book starts bulging at the seams.

I'll also be getting on to marketing in this lesson too. A quick-fire double punch of core concepts to digest, which will hopefully stay with you forever. Let's say you had £1 billion worth of gold bars in your back garden. You are trying to sell them at £1 a pop and you wait all day, but no one comes to buy one, despite it being a complete and utter bargain.

Unless you advertise and market the fact, or have established contacts, you won't sell one bar. Marketing could be in the form of neon signs leading the way, putting up the information online, calling your contacts or even just telling one person – which will then likely turn into word-of-mouth promotion.

Marketing is such a key component for resale and yet so many people don't understand it properly or make simple mistakes that would be easy to avoid. I will give you the tools to market effectively when it comes to resale to help you sell items and maximize profits.

BUILDING CONTACTS IS KEY

Having different contacts for niche items and genres is great as it will mean having someone to sell to instantly. But how do you build these contacts? Let's take an antiques shop setting as an example. When you enter and that little bell jingles above your head, you're accomplishing two different things without knowing it.

Your intention is to seek out items to turn a profit. But you are also collecting data in your resale memory bank to use at a later date. Perhaps you see that someone is a massive collector of, let's say, musical instruments. You step inside this person's shop, take a look around and build a rapport with the owner, even if you don't buy anything. Later down the line, you can potentially call them, remind that person of how you met and then tap them for knowledge.

In the future, it's as easy as sending a text message photograph to that dealer when you come across an instrument, asking what they would pay for it. Can you make a profit? What you're doing is pre-selling items before you even purchase them.

This is another example of mitigating risk, because you won't need to worry when you are going to sell that item, how much you'll be able to sell it for and who will buy it. You've already established that before the money comes out of your pocket.

Nobody could ever memorize the value of every single item ever created and it's just not necessary. Not if you allow someone else or something else – a website, an app or a specialist dealer – to do the work for you. You do not need to have that knowledge yourself.

You just need to focus on gathering those resources and those contacts to give you that information – you'd go crazy trying to appraise thousands of items. I make it as easy as possible by making someone or something else do the work.

It is also worth having a notepad and pen with you at all times. You can take notes of stock in different shops, go home and do the research to identify the bargains, then come back to take advantage.

DON'T BURN BRIDGES

When you start getting into speciality items, you'll come across the same people – again and again –and you may well communicate with a buyer even after your transaction is over. It has happened thousands of times in my career: I've sold an item to someone then contacted them later to sell them even more. It's about flexibility in resale and gaining information from people on what they're after. It's about maintaining those bridges, not burning them.

Sometimes, a buyer or seller doesn't particularly want cash – or need the cash to buy something else. If you're willing to trade an item for more items, it can be advantageous for all concerned. I would always recommend that the other item, or the multiple items, have a higher value.

In some circumstances, this can be better than taking a discounted price in cash when you sell an item. If you get the cash, you have to spend more time looking for other items to reinvest the money and make a profit on, increasing your workload and reducing your potential earnings. Remember, you need to work out your hourly wage – even with an item swap.

This is all quite basic, but very important when it comes to resale. Introduce yourself and try to remember the names of people you buy and sell with. As you come across the same people more and more, at the very least you will get a better deal as a repeat customer. Best case scenario, you could make a new resale friend.

RESALE MUSCLE MEMORY

In the long term, building contacts also helps you gain experience and collect data. You can learn from these people. Essentially, you know there's a strong chance that you're going to run across a similar item again. Soon it becomes a resale muscle memory, like knowing the price of a litre of unleaded or a pint of milk.

For example: I've already made two quid from item A. If I come across it again, next week or three months down the line, I won't have to think about it – it's in my knowledge bank and I know I can make two quid easily. You can grab the item and move on to the next thing. That experience is in your brain – your resale muscle memory. You want to start acquiring those items.

If you gain that experience, you become more efficient and you become faster, which in turn leads to more money in your pocket.

THE SIX DEGREES OF RESALE BACON

Every meeting with someone is an opportunity to market an item – even if you're conversing with them about a completely different item. Let's say you're selling a gardening item to someone. While that transaction is going ahead, you say, 'I'm also selling a car at the moment, just in case you're interested'.

You're connecting the dots because everybody knows somebody. That person might not want the car but might say, 'Oh, well, actually my buddy is in the market for a motor'. Or, 'I saw a friend of a friend on Facebook say they're after a new set of wheels.'

Whoever you are talking to – whether it's your parents, boss or barista, whoever it might be – what you're trying to do is shift another item. It works best if the item is of the same ilk. So, if you're selling a lawnmower, perhaps your buyer might also be interested in some shears or a shovel.

It's so important to ask questions, to see whether or not the buyer knows anyone that could be looking for something that you're trying to sell. Many sellers are reluctant to do this but you're missing out on the potential for more sales straight away.

Going back to the radio tubes, I had a tough time finding a buyer because they are niche items. Eventually I managed to find a buyer who deals with vintage audio equipment. While I was dealing with the radio tubes, I told him about that rare RCA 44-BX microphone I mentioned in the last lesson.

He said, 'I'm not a music guy, but I know a guy that I sell to.' Because sure enough, amplifiers and other vintage musical recording equipment use antique tubes. My buyer and this new buyer network but deal in two completely different things. He gave me his contact details, I gave him a buzz. The very next day I sold him that microphone. And that was just by laying out what I had and asking questions.

Right then and there, you're already generating sales, whether or not the person you're speaking to is actually your customer. It could be someone that they know. That's what you're trying to do – follow a path to your customer, whether it's the second person along, the third or the fourth.

It's like the ongoing joke, the Six Degrees of Kevin Bacon. Everyone is six people away from knowing actor Kevin Bacon. In resale, you're trying to identify six degrees of your customer or six degrees of a sale. Within six people, you will be able to identify someone who wants to buy whatever you're trying to sell. Just to manage your expectations, it's unlikely to actually *be* Kevin Bacon.

SOMEONE HERE WILL BUY YOUR ITEM

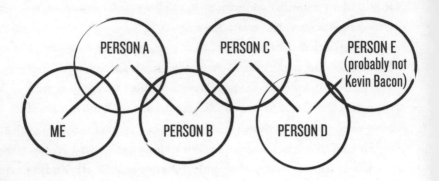

SELL YOURSELF! IT'S ALL ABOUT THAT REPEAT CUSTOMER

While you are establishing those contacts and building those bridges, you are not so much selling your items as selling yourself. You're establishing yourself as a legitimate seller.

Your goal is this: if you're able to acquire that item again, or something similar, you need to have established a repeat customer. Some of my biggest buyers in the antiques business are repeat customers.

You might never find a radio tube, for example, again. But if you happen to come across more radio tubes out in the wild, you already have the contact established. It was worth building that bridge. What you're doing is becoming a radio tube salesman – and whenever you see these things again, wherever you are, you know you can buy and sell them quickly for a profit.

Without knowing it, you're establishing yourself as a legitimate seller to that person for that specific item. I have a guy that I go to when I find radio tubes, I have a guy to go for my general antiques, for my sports cards, for my video games, for my car and automobile antiques. There's someone to go to for everything in that niche market, and you want to find the person that fits each category. So when you go to a thrift store or car boot sale, there will be 50 things you can identify that you already have a buyer for. You're not selling the particular item, you're selling yourself as the legitimate seller and the platform for someone else to come to, for them to acquire the thing that they're after.

Now I can spot radio tubes from 100 yards away. I would never have looked at them before. I keep my eye out to find more because I know I can just sell them on to this guy. Because I have sold him good-quality radio tubes already, and I've always been professional, on time, good at contacting back and forth and polite, it means I've built a great contact. He knows I'm reliable for next time and it cuts down the selling time considerably.

I can literally have an item in my hands for seconds before I pass it on for a flipping profit. I am Jesse McClure, Resale King. But to that specific buyer, I am Jesse McClure, Radio Tube Salesman.

IF YOU MARKET IT, THEY WILL COME

Alongside building contacts, correct marketing is one of the most important aspects of resale. I've met some of the greatest used-car salespeople in the world. But for them to open their own car dealership would be pointless, because they wouldn't know the first thing about drawing the custom in. If a customer appeared, they could sell them a car, but going out to find that customer and bringing them to the dealership is a different set of skills. It requires marketing.

One of the simplest forms of marketing is the sign, or billboard in the US. There's a reason why billboards are a billion-dollar industry. If you're creating your own billboard – a glorified sign made with a permanent marker and paper, for example – you'll want to put it in the right place.

If you're selling at a car boot sale, you won't necessarily have to put up signs, but the way you set up your spot can determine whether you draw customers in, based on what they see in that first two seconds of glancing at your space.

You want to focus on where people are going, and how you can put your name out there to be noticed by that foot traffic, like putting up a sign in the street. The most high-traffic area at a car boot sale is usually at the entrance or at a corner. Grab that spot and you know that they're going to see you from all angles – they're going to peek at your stuff, whether they like it or not. There are plenty of subtle little tricks like this.

WHERE DO YOUR EYES GO?

If you identify where people's eyes go, you can help manipulate sales. In the supermarket, you know where the bread is going to be found, the milk and so on. These shops are all largely formatted in the same way. However, when you stroll down an aisle, your eyes will naturally fall on the middle shelf. Because of this, the middle shelf is usually where they put the priciest stuff. Your eyes tend not to fall on the top or bottom shelf while you browse.

You can use this methodology in resale: where are the eyes naturally going to go? What you're doing is passively marketing to people, whether they are after your stuff or not, because their eyes are naturally going to be drawn in that general direction.

I'll go back to the gold bar analogy – if you're at a car boot sale and you're selling a gold bar for a pound, if it's buried under a load of items that people won't care about, it won't get sold. It's about making sure that all your best items are in the middle so people can see what you're all about.

There's a reason why clothing shops display their best and newest stuff in the front, and their clearance and sale stuff at the back. You want to emulate that same exact thing – extract the knowledge and experience these large corporations have, they have entire marketing teams working on it. Don't waste your time trying to create your own marketing strategy and plan, use other companies' tactics. They're paying for their own marketing team, you can use the information for free. Gather all those ideas – whether it's a billboard, an in-store sign or a promotion that jumps out – take notes and ask yourself, 'How can I apply that to my own resale business to acquire customers and sales?'

ACTION POINT: Think about the last few shops you've been in. What are the best marketing tricks you've seen? Jot them down and use them in your resale adventure. Free marketing advice, see.

TRADITIONAL VERSUS NEW-GENERATION MARKETING

In recent years, opportunities for marketing items have changed vastly, creating two types of seller. There's the traditional seller, who doesn't really use the internet to market items, and the new-generation seller, who does. I'm more of a traditional seller, but I like to blend the two approaches, depending on the circumstances.

Social media has become a huge platform for resale. For example,

Instagram is full of people selling vintage clothes and other fashion items. The advantage is that these clothes can be made to look great on a model, or however the photograph has been staged, and it will make someone want to buy them.

But, for me, this is the equivalent of opening a window in your home and yelling out to the whole world, 'Buy my stuff!' It's not direct enough. What you want to do is connect with your network of friends and family, especially in the very beginning. What this does is passively set up a customer base with little effort.

It's important to ask questions before you start to buy. What are your friends looking for? Don't sell to friends and family, BUY FOR friends and family. Bad things usually happen when you try to sell them stuff randomly – think of those multi-level marketing schemes: how many people do you know spamming your social media selling health shakes, candles or other such goods? How much does it annoy you? See.

Naturally, these will be the first sales that you generate, whether it's a friendly gesture or they really do want your product. Establish these sales first, then connect with their friends and family to repeat the cycle. It's so much easier to start growing organically in this way. It can be a mistake, both in terms of money and time, if you start by only trying to sell your items to the general public on the internet. Although, in the beginning, this approach can still be a solid avenue for sales, especially if you use commission-free platforms such as Facebook.

ACTION POINT: Try it out. Ask a friend or family member if they are looking to buy something specific, and how much they are willing to pay for it. Then, go out and find it cheaper. Use the tips we have shown you so far to find a price lower than they are willing to pay, then pocket the profits. Or, make them feel good and let them enjoy the unexpected discount while you enjoy the success of your new-found bargaining skills.

FIND THE RIGHT MARKET (LIKE POPEYE!)

To hammer home this point again, it is all about identifying the right place to sell – whether it's a specific customer you have already sold to, a website, a specialist company or a specialist platform. The right choice is key.

Recently, I went through the process of auctioning off a multitude of different items. The easy solution would be to box them all up and send them to one general auction house. They would just auction off the lot, irrelevant of what the items are. That, however, wouldn't maximize profits or get the right eyes on the items.

If I have automobile items, I send them to an auction house that specializes in automobile items – they auction off the vintage car brochures and car parts I have. All my Disney collectibles head to a place called Potter and Potters in Chicago, as I have used them before and I know they have the right buyers to make chunky profits. You need to seek out these auction houses, because they have a customer base for a specific item or genre. What you're doing is using their long-established specific customer base to maximize your profit potential.

It takes a little bit more work to sell through a number of different routes, so you need to decide, once again, if it is worth your time to eke out the profits. If you send all your items to a general auction, you're going to have people just hunting for value. Let's say, looking at the items you have, you could make £1,000 with ease. However, you could separate them out and find speciality selling options across the country, with a bit of Googling, and make £5,000 instead. It is of course then well worth that extra effort.

It's the difference between boxing and shipping ten things and putting on the same address label, or boxing up the same ten things and putting on ten different address labels. It shouldn't take more than a couple of hours and a few emails to some of these auction houses or platforms to establish some of the different values that they're getting for items, but remember to factor in your time. Keep track of your time to make sure you're getting good value for money – and you can refer back to this as you do it more to realize which items are worth separating out this way, and which aren't.

Let me give you an example: I had an original 1982 Popeye Nintendo arcade system in my antiques mall for six months, priced at $1,300. This is a game steeped in history, launching between the iconic Donkey Kong and Mario Bros arcade games that swept North America by storm in the early 80s. Despite this, and the fact it was in pristine condition and in an eye-catching sky blue, just one person was interested in it. They offered me $800 and I almost took it.

Instead, that offer prompted me into action, like Popeye. Realizing the item had triggered my six-month expiry date, I decided to put in the extra time and found an arcade auction house in Anaheim, California. I drove an hour to put it to auction. It sold for a whopping $4,000.

That arcade machine was too niche to sell in a general antiques mall, but that auction could offer me an existing customer base of arcade enthusiasts. In turn, my profit grew three-fold. Just by taking that extra time – all it took was a Google search for 'auction house that sells arcade games' – I found exactly what I was looking for in a matter of minutes.

Taking my Popeye example, Google is the spinach. Make sure you eat it to flex those profit muscles. Hey, even I'm still learning every day.

DON'T FORGET INVENTORY CONTROL

Taking that example above, I'd had that machine for half a year and I realized that was too long. I had to find an alternative way to get it off the shelf and that lowball bid was my trigger. What this also highlights is that you've got to practise inventory control. People get caught up when they start saying it is worth this much, or that much.

The prime example is you can pick up any price guide book and it can say an item's worth £10,000. In reality, an item is only worth what someone is willing to pay for it in the current market. It doesn't matter what the guide says it is worth. Do your own research and take guides with a pinch of salt.

Take Beanie Babies and the fad that exploded in the late 1990s. Look at what a price guide says certain ones sell for and then compare the price people are actually paying for them. Two completely different things. You need to establish a happy medium: how can I maximize both my time and profit, without getting caught up in the 'true value'.

You don't want to be stuck with an item for months on end, just taking up time and space. This is space that could and should be used for something new so that you keep churning profit.

Don't get trapped by FOMO (fear of missing out). No really, don't get caught up on what the value of an item used to be or what you think it is worth. Still don't believe me? Bitcoin was $18,500 a coin when I wrote this. Feel free to look it up now. Up or down, I'm fairly certain the price is…well, different.

WHAT ABOUT MARKETING STUNTS?

I don't go down this route too much. I never waste the most valuable thing I own – my time. On the whole, marketing stunts shouldn't be needed. If you've already done all the groundwork, the desperation to sell an item via a stunt should be minimal. However, there is one stunt I do occasionally perform, just to give an example.

You get to a car boot sale at 6am. You unload all your stuff and from 7am to 2pm, the aim is to sell as much stuff as you can. As I've already mentioned, nobody really wants to come home with any of those items. They're selling at a car boot sale for a reason.

I have price points for all my items. Every hour, I'll lower the price on an item until it's gone. I've done this a handful of times and managed to sell every single thing on my spot. I went home with nothing. It is possible.

If it's your goal to get rid of everything, some stuff is going to go cheap. But would you rather go home with an extra five quid in your pocket, or take the item back with you? If you're going to throw it away or donate it if you don't sell, you might as well get as much as you can for it. Establish that starting point and establish that end point. You can have the sliding scale of discount going on until it gets to 90 per cent off. Don't marry items – see it as clearing stock for the next thing.

These tricks do work with people who believe they are getting a bargain. There's a reason why Poundland is thriving in the UK and Dollar Tree is in the US. They largely contain stuff that other shops couldn't sell and that you don't really need – but it looks like such a bargain. That's where they get you.

TAKE ADVANTAGE OF POOR MARKETING – THE $500 BASKETBALL

I can't tell you the number of times I've seen sellers do the exact opposite of what I'm conveying in this chapter, and I've taken advantage of the situation. You don't always need to think in terms of how can I market this better? Sometimes it's as simple as how can I make this look better? I once made a huge profit on a basketball because someone didn't take the time to do that.

The ball was signed by Kobe Bryant and was listed for $200 right after he passed away. The seller was looking to make money on Black Mamba's sad passing and take advantage of the opportunity. I scooped it up straight away, knowing I could make money on it – it was priced low because the ball was deflated and because the seller had no paperwork to prove the signature.

What I did was to check out some of these grading services – not only do they give you a certificate of authenticity (which was missing for this particular ball), but they also put a hologram sticker on the item to identify it. That tiny sticker on the ball shows a company name and a serial number. Now if you do a tiny bit of Googling – just a tiny bit – you can call the company, pay $10 and they'll send you a replacement certificate of authenticity.

I inflated the ball with a $5 pump that I already had and paid an extra $10 to get a Perspex case to put it in. I sold that ball for $500 – doubling my outlay.

I didn't have to do much. I just put it back out there, but made it look nicer. It's a metaphor for *Never Go Broke* – literally pumping up profits with a little extra energy, effort and care.

This is exactly what car sellers do. They buy a nearly new motor, polish it up, make it look shiny and new and glean a bit of profit on it. I have seen it far too many times. If you sell your car, give it a wash.

You are far more likely to sell a clean car than a dirty one. It's obvious, but it's often overlooked.

ACTION POINT: What do you have at home that can be cleaned up and sold for profit like a car? Replace the word 'car' with whatever you happen to be flogging. Sometimes the most important tool you can have in selling is a washrag and spray bottle.

KEY POINTS TO RECAP

- Having a contacts book is key – it'll help you get expert advice quickly and sell items on, pronto.
- Make sure you treat your contacts with care to build up a rapport. You'll never know when you might need them.
- All the time, the idea is to collect information and experience – remember that as you get further into resale.
- Find your Kevin Bacon. Your buyer is only a contact – or a contact of a contact – away.
- The easiest sale is to a repeat customer who will trust you to deliver the goods.
- Make sure you market your items effectively by signposting.
- It's no good trying to sell a bar of gold for $1 if the correct eyes don't see it.
- Marketing and building contacts get the right people ready to buy. It's better than the internet crapshoot.
- Find the right place to market and sell your item. Take your time to establish where this will be.
- You'll need some inventory control. You don't want to be left with a pile of items you can't shift.
- You shouldn't need to use marketing stunts – your items should largely sell themselves.
- Don't sell yourself short with rubbish marketing. If in doubt, think about the Kobe basketball.

LESSON 10: SPOTTING TRENDS AND RECOGNIZING PATTERNS

Spotting trends is all about following consumer spending behaviour and patterns, and knowing when to strike. It is far easier than you think.

However, we don't have a crystal ball. We cannot tell you what item is going to be hot next week, next month or next year. It's changing all the time. But there are some ways to spot these future trends using social media, diving into Google Trends, trawling data to establish the next 'hot thing'.

The idea is to buy items halfway up the hill, to sell on at the top of the hill, before the hill starts to slope downwards. As the world continues to move and adapt in a technological age, people have more power than ever before to read data and attempt to get 'ahead of the curve'. That said, when it comes to patterns, some have been readable since the dawn of time.

We're going to explain how and why it is so important to keep an ear to the ground, and how to buy items with minimal effort that will then grow hot.

FIND THE SELLING SWEET SPOT

As more people start to collect an item and more – or less – of those items become available, a price trend occurs.

Some items have crazy value and some will never see the beauty that is a comma in a price. But that's irrelevant – you need to understand that every single item has a 'value-trend'. An item can be at its highest popularity or at its lowest popularity it can be at its highest value or its lowest value.

These things are not mutually exclusive – an item can be at its highest popularity but its least value at the same time, often thanks to market saturation. The idea is to find that sweet spot where an item's highest value and its highest popularity coincide. That is the time to sell.

POPULARITY PROFIT HILL

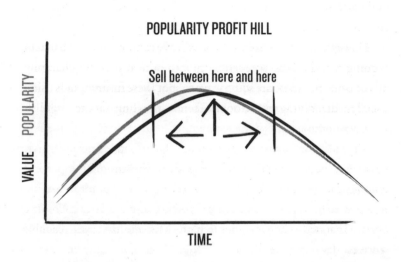

Sell between here and here

POPULARITY

VALUE

TIME

RECOGNIZING PATTERNS

The idea behind recognizing patterns is to do your best to enter a market at the 'right' time – and exit at the 'right' time too. That could be selling stocks, cryptocurrency, Beanie Babies, video games or antique furniture – you name it.

For example, when a movie comes out and it is popular, people tend to want to buy anything related to it. Let's say it's a superhero flick and, suddenly, everyone is interested in *Marvel* memorabilia. Lee has a great example of this. Having followed with interest the graphic novel series *The Boys* a few years ago, he was talking to his friend about the fact it had been picked up by Amazon Prime for a television show, after years of rumours about it being made into a Hollywood flick.

Shortly after that conversation, his friend travelled to Canada and, as luck would have it, spotted the first graphic novel of *The Boys* in a thrift store window, signed by the author and illustrator. It was priced at $15 and he bought it, thanks to his recent conversation with Lee.

A few months later the show aired, was immensely popular and now the graphic novel has a huge new set of fans. With a second series airing and its popularity soaring, the first signed edition of the comic could be worth ten times what he paid for it. Some examples are selling on eBay for more than £100. It's a classic example of keeping an eye out for future releases and trying to capitalize on a likely surge in interest.

In the finance sector, precious metals such as gold and silver go in and out of vogue depending on economic factors around the globe. In 1636 in Amsterdam, Holland, there was a mad frenzy for tulips. The price of bulbs went through the roof before spectacularly collapsing. In recent times, cryptocurrencies such as Bitcoin have seen a similar pattern. There will be winners, of course, but also many losers in all of those examples.

It is all about behavioural finance and recognizing patterns. Remember when Pogs went big in the 90s? They were just cardboard discs but some of the prices went mad. In those early stages of a craze – whether it is Pogs or Pokémon cards – there is money to be made, but you have to exit pretty swiftly to keep the profits. Unless, of course, they come back into fashion further down the line, but that's difficult to predict.

If you get in at a certain point and exit at a certain point, you're more likely to make a profit. But we're not psychics so we don't know when those exact points are. If we did we'd be millionaires on the stock market. The idea is to start recognizing patterns so you're not stuck with 10,000 fidget spinners or Beanie Babies further down the line.

Believe me, I have learned that the hard way. It's not all been sunshine and kittens.

DON'T BECOME THE BAG HOLDER

The idea of recognizing patterns is to position yourself so you don't become the bag holder. This is essentially the person left holding the bill at the end of an adventure. Back in the day when I was with all my high-school friends, we'd go out to eat at a diner chain called Denny's. The idea – if there were six of us – was to be one of the first five to escape, leaving the sixth guy to pay the entire bill. (I'm not going to confirm or deny whether that actually ever happened.)

Recognizing patterns is really about behavioural finance – one of my favourite topics. Essentially, behavioural finance looks to understand why people make certain financial choices, whether they actually make sense or not. In this case, you can be the most successful when you have enough self-awareness to remove yourself from pop culture fads and holidays at the right time.

The easiest pattern to recognize is Christmas, which has been around every year since the beginning of capitalism. There's a hot item every year that people go out and buy for the kids, whether it's a Tickle Me Elmo, a Beanie Baby, a video game, board game or book – or Turbo Man from Schwarzenegger flick *Jingle All The Way*. What you're doing is recognizing a pattern as it creates demand and triggers scarcity.

The pattern here is that people are willing to pay more money for an item just before Christmas, simply because there's a deadline they have to hit. In this case it's Christmas Day so the present can be tucked under the tree and the kids can open it, creating (probably short-lived) happiness. The idea is not only to be aware of these particular patterns, but also not get yourself involved – when you do, you risk becoming the bag holder.

I'll give you a specific story. When the PlayStation 3 came out just before Christmas 2006, I was living in Los Angeles and it coincided with Black Friday. I found out through various connections that a Best Buy store in a town called Carson City, Nevada, had three of them available on Black Friday. I waited in line from 6pm until 7am.

I was third in the queue and ready to go but I had made a critical error in my hastiness. I had left the heat of LA to come to a town where the temperature dropped, and I was in shorts and flip-flops! When Best Buy opened, I ran in like I was appearing on television show *Supermarket Sweep*. I knocked over a whole display of Jay Z albums, but I got my hands on those consoles. My dogged determination paid off. The idea was to keep one and sell two, but in the end I sold all three.

When I first had them, they were selling on average for three times the original purchase price – around $1,000 each. But as more people became aware, everyone began flooding the secondary market and listing them online. I sold the first for $950, a serious profit. The second one I didn't sell until the week before Christmas, and I received $850.

But that's when things became trickier, as I still had the third one and Christmas was fast approaching. I made the conscious decision to let it go for a smaller profit or risk being stuck with it – I knew that after Christmas Day, PlayStation would go back to its retail value. To avoid becoming a bag holder, I ended up selling the third one for $490 – still a profit.

When you recognize a pattern, you also have to recognize an expiry date on potential opportunities as they come – and that can happen quickly. For example, if you have an old smartphone, the next model is going to come out soon – every day, the price drops. You have to make a conscious decision to find the balance between turning a profit and moving on to the next thing, and being so adamant about getting a certain price for it that you get stuck with it. Becoming the bag holder and not turning a profit will be the result of your own stubbornness.

Also, don't fall into the game of mass buying a specific item. I really do know someone who bought 10,000 fidget spinners at a few cents each when they were selling for $3 a pop. That fad lived and died so fast that the guy still has 9,750 fidget spinners. He's the metaphorical bag holder in my Denny's tale.

DON'T BE MICHAEL FISH!

Okay, let's imagine you've got a small stall selling items to punters on the street. Suddenly the weather turns nasty (not difficult to imagine in Britain) and it's raining cats and dogs. It's completely unexpected. Now, on that stall, you have a secret stash of umbrellas and you become the only person selling them on that street and you have no competition. You turn your stall over to umbrellas.

This is not pigeonholing yourself, but understanding the opportunity and how you can take advantage of it. Pigeonholing yourself in that scenario would be still trying to sell umbrellas in the dead heat of summer. But you're smarter than that. You have a secret stash of sunscreen, and you are now flipping your focus.

Weatherman Michael Fish infamously said in 1987 that he'd heard reports of a hurricane about to hit Britain. He stated on national television that the claims were false. Then the hurricane hit. You need to be adaptable and accept that, sometimes, the climate can change pretty rapidly even if you're not expecting it and have all the data in the world.

The moral of the story is understanding the timeframe and the opportunities, and milking the situation for everything it has got. Invest smartly, but never overinvest in case it comes back and blows up in your face, like a fish in a hurricane.

HOW DO YOU SPOT THE GAP?

So, how do you spot a gap in a particular market if you're an antiques dealer, selling at car boot sales or making a one-off sale? How do you take advantage?

Here's an example of an antiques dealer I know in a nearby mall. This guy – let's call him Jerry – is in his 60s and has retired recently as a prison guard. He's only just got into antiques. He was putting various knick-knacks and miscellaneous items into his booth but business wasn't going great.

One day, on a whim, he ordered in a few gemstones for his stand – your run-of-the-mill amethyst, jade and topaz. People went wild for them and he was selling out on a frequent basis so he ordered bigger quantities. Now, instead of just riding that wave, he recognized he had a customer base looking for gemstones – so he expanded into jewellery. Bigger rocks to turn bigger profits.

He had identified an opportunity to acknowledge a gap in the market. In this circumstance, the gap was that no one else was selling gemstones in that antiques mall, and there were customers looking for those things. Jerry was able to start researching and learning about gemstones and before long he was making an extra thousand dollars a month, simply by recognizing the gap that no one else had spotted.

It's trial by error – and when that error comes good, it's about further exploiting the opportunity and swotting up on research to maximize it further.

In the context of a car boot sale, for example, it might mean going to the sale the week beforehand to you selling to see what everyone else is flogging. How are you going to stand out? How are you going to have a Jerry moment?

One of the biggest issues and ways I see people fail is they don't do their 'market research' or suss out the competition. I've seen so many sellers over the years with amazing antiques, but they don't have an eye on their rivals – and they hardly sell a thing. They'll ask me why it is happening. I'll ask them if they've taken a lap around and seen the competition.

A shake of their head confirms a major error – sometimes a few spaces down from them, there'll be another antiques dealer selling nearly the same thing, but for 10–30 per cent less. You have to understand the customer will simply go and buy the same items for cheaper, just like my Tommy Hilfiger luggage example.

If you don't recognize who else is out there and selling something similar to you, you're not going to be able to compete. It's the foundation for being successful, rather than failing and not knowing why.

ACTION POINT: The next time you go to your local car boot sale, ask yourself what this place is not selling that is needed? Could you reasonably fill that niche?

DON'T SNOW THE SNOWMAN

I use this saying frequently – for me, it means ignore the obvious and find non-speciality items at speciality stores. Taking advantage of speciality sellers who are selling items that fall out of their wheelhouse is a worthwhile endeavour. For example, buying vintage electronics from a vintage clothing seller. Or buying non-tools from a tool guy.

I'll give you an example. Just now I revealed how I queued up overnight in my flip-flops to bag some PS3s. Well, I did something similar with Nintendo Wii. Those consoles saw a meteoric rise in popularity and everybody and their dog wanted one. I found a certain store that sold a few electronics, but it wasn't known for selling electronics – and it enabled me to turn a hot profit.

The weekend the Wii came out, I headed for Sam's Club, a cut-price wholesaler best known for its sales of bulk food – 5kg boxes of Coco Pops and the like. Tucked away at the back was a small electronics section. I didn't even have to queue up overnight for this haul – I simply thought outside the box, headed down there at opening time and, to my delight, found ten Wiis for sale. I bought them all. I could have Wiied in excitement (sorry). I was able to take advantage because people headed for the obvious spots to buy them, like video game stores where I knew I would have competition.

In terms of selling, I was able to identify a large swap meet known for its higher-priced items and I sold them there. It was getting close to the holidays – the prime time to sell electronics. I could have probably got more if I'd sat on them, put them on eBay and shipped them. But it's a judgement call. Sometimes you want to shift things while they're hot.

I offloaded them for a 50-per-cent mark-up as opposed to, say, a 75-per-cent mark-up. But I had to evaluate my time and effort, listing and shipping ten consoles individually as opposed to a one-day sell-a-thon. I had ten consoles, and that 50-per-cent profit made it very worthwhile indeed.

The Nintendo Wii was released in November 2006, and I had just turned the ripe old age of 20. Grab an opportunity while you can, but don't be like greedy, young Jesse, who tried to price gauge poor young kids who wanted a Nintendo from Father Christmas. Shame on you young Jesse…shame.

KEY POINTS TO RECAP

- Look for that selling sweet spot and try to pre-empt it.
- Always think about what is happening in the near or distant future, so you can buy low and sell high when popularity starts to spike.
- The most obvious pattern? Christmas. Ask yourself how you can exploit an annual event like this to make bumper profits.
- Don't be a bag holder and put all of your eggs in one basket. You could be left with a huge pile of fidget spinners.
- You may need to flip your focus, depending on the time of year.
- Adapt and do things differently. You might need to look at a different genre or niche to keep making profits, like Jerry did.
- Look for items in a specialist store that the store doesn't specialize in – you might be able to exploit their ignorance.

END OF PART II

By now you must be itching to get to Part III where I reveal to you all the places you can buy items to flip for profits. Before we do that, I want you to take a deep breath and really soak in the lessons you've learned. Repeat after me:

Everything REALLY does have value.
There are MANY traps to avoid when it comes to resale – especially looking for that diamond in the rough.
It is better to focus on those SMALL GAINS first of all.
Your time is PRECIOUS and you'll want to maximize it.
Building a CONTACT BOOK is key.
MARKETING correctly is also key.
Spotting TRENDS is easy.
Spotting PATTERNS is even easier.

Remember, the key recaps at the end of every lesson are there for you to peruse before diving headfirst into imagining yourself rummaging at a car boot sale, walking down an autumnal English street laced with antiques shops or combing those charity shop clothes rails.

At the end of Part I, there was a progress report for you to fill in. Part II has an ideas page. This is a safe space to jot down some notes. What could your bread-and-butter items potentially be? What niches are you thinking about looking into? What patterns and trends are likely to emerge in the next year or two? Where are you going to buy your shiny new contacts book from and what colour will it be? You can lay it all down in this space.

JOT YOUR OWN BLUEPRINT NOTES HERE:

PART III:

PRACTICAL PLACES TO BAG PROFITS

Resale is a rollercoaster – you've just got to ride it.

You've made it to the last section of the book. Hopefully, by now, you've followed the advice in Part I and built up a pot of cash for reinvestment, and established your blueprint for resale after reading Part II.

In Part III, we'll list all the best places to find bargains and flip them for tidy – and sometimes bumper – profits. Some of these ideas may seem basic, but it's important to re-evaluate opportunities as trends, platforms and buying habits change. I went from hardcore international antiques guy to hipster vintage clothing kid and I keep evolving like a resale chameleon.

We'll take you on a rollercoaster ride of car boot sales, estate sales, speciality auctions, storage auctions, antiques markets and charity shops.

Are you strapped in? Let's go!

LESSON 11: CAR BOOT SALES AND SWAP MEETS – BE FIRST (OR LAST)

LEVEL: Beginner
PROFIT POTENTIAL: £££

Oh boy, do we love a car boot sale. The dew on early morning grass. The plethora of colourful characters that turn up from nowhere to an obscure field on the hunt for treasure. The smell of fried onions…and ripe bargains ready to be plucked from the juicy tree of boot.

The 'booty' has stalls of the weird, wonderful and everything in between. We have found some utter bargains at these meets – and honestly, you can too. In the US, there are similar events: we call them swap meets. In this first specific lesson about buying and selling, we will guide you through the basics in order to bag top looty at a booty to sell on for profit.

It's not an easy task if you go in blind. The vast majority of wares on offer are unlikely to flip a profit – but it's safe to say there is still the opportunity to find untapped gems. And it can deliver one huge jolt of adrenaline. You'll just need to have a sharp eye and apply some of what you've learned from previous lessons.

Here we let you in on some of our expert tricks and tips – and reveal why it pays to be first, or last, through the gates at these beloved events.

WHAT IS IT? THE ESSENTIALS

Car boot sales and swap meets are often found dotted around the land at weekends, usually with a break over winter – no one wants to be buying or selling in a muddy, cold, wet field – although there's a growing trend for year-round, indoor events.

There is usually a small entry fee to get in to buy and a bigger one to have a stall to sell. Scientific research (yes, really) suggests they are vital to the economy, with the rotation of household goods essential for preventing waste and disposal costs.

Car boot sales were popularized in the 1970s, usually as charity-based events in local communities. However, as households began to grow and consume cheaper goods, they became a quick way to shift unwanted items. Britons now spend around £1.5 billion a year at car boot sales. It's a huge money-making opportunity.

WHY IT'S WORTH YOUR TIME

Around half of sellers are novices who are simply decluttering their homes. This is usually the last step before they head to the tip to dispose of the junk they no longer want, gathering dust around their property.

In a time when tidy homes have become a new 'fad', people are willing to get rid of goods at a rock-bottom price to ditch the clutter. We can partly thank Japanese cleaning whizz Marie Kondo for this.

Buying from novices can mean two things: firstly, they may not realize that an item or two of their junk is worth way more than they think – whether it has been handed down, inherited or just grown in value without them cottoning on. If you have a keen eye, it is easy to spot these items with huge profitability and we will tell you how.

Secondly, they are unlikely to be comfortable haggling and really do not want to lug their junk home. That means you can drive them to low prices, safe in the knowledge that they are keen to offload.

The other sellers at car boot sales are veterans or professionals of the car boot circuit. You'll be best targeting the novices.

PROFIT POTENTIAL

The profits on offer at car boot sales can be substantial. If you visited one with £50 in your pocket, there is an opportunity to turn that into at least a five-fold profit. That's what we'd aim for.

One of the easiest scores is multimedia, as we outline below. I once turned $15 into $200 in an afternoon by simply buying boxes of CDs and DVDs, which I could see were in good condition. I've also turned $500 of boombox buys – now a staple for me when I visit car boot sales – into at least a ten-fold profit. And remember earlier when I said I'm always on the lookout for Leica cameras when at a car boot sale? Well that has made me some juicy profits too.

I treat multimedia as my bread and butter, and boomboxes and Leica cameras as a niche I've carved that I know is likely to turn profit thanks to experience. You can find your bread and butter, and some speciality niche items, and you'll be setting the groundwork to make sure you'll never go broke.

Just to get you inspired...a lady at a boot sale a few years ago took a £25 punt on a 6-inch tall figure, because she had a 'good feeling about it'. It transpired to be a rare 16th-century statue of the Tibetan goddess Green Tara – it sold for £15,500 shortly afterwards at auction.

The figure was on a table of bric-a-brac. This highlights the profitability lurking at some of these events – and also that you should trust your gut. The lady was quoted as saying, 'You should always keep your eyes open at things like car boot sales – there is a chance you could pick up a statue like this one.'

The key, for me, is to look at an item like this, inspect it closely, walk away, try to research it with your phone, then go for it. Even though finds like the above are rare, you've got to be in it to win it – if it ends up being a dud, you'll still be able to recoup some or all of your money, or even make a small profit. You can be overly cautious.

HOW TO FIND A GOOD CAR BOOT SALE

There are websites online that list car boot sales across the country (see the Resources at the end of this lesson). The best ones have website links to see the details – if you're going there looking to sniff out a bargain, the bigger the boot sale the better, simply because more wares will be on offer.

Outdoor car boot sales are what most people are used to, but these tend to close between October and March, simply because of the weather and the chances of a waterlogged field. However, there are indoor versions. Often these are hybrids – if the weather is good, it'll be in a village hall car park, for example, but if the weather is bad, it'll be indoors. There are some that are outdoors all year round, usually in car parks.

It is worth asking people for the best boot sale they've been to. You'll be surprised what friends get up to at the weekend and they might have a top tip for you.

Most boot sales ask for a nominal fee to enter – usually around 50p. Just make sure you hand over a 50p that is not rare or collectible (see page 49)! Whether you're buying or selling, go with a mix of cash: bank notes and coins. A backpack and carrier bags are also a must.

ACTION POINT: Research the car boot sales local to you – when they start, entry prices – and mark on your calendar your first planned Never Go Broke car boot raid.

Tips and tricks for success

1. Be a locust to make profit

'If you ain't first, you're last,' so said the great (fictional) Ricky Bobby in cult film *Talladega Nights*. Arrive early at a boot sale and you have first dibs on all the good stuff. However, sellers really do hate locusts that start to hassle them at the starting gun as they try to carefully organize their goods into some sort of order to be appealing to buyers.

But, in terms of opportunity, you can play into the mindset of: I'm offering you cold cash for this right away, and you might not get a better offer all day. Also, getting that first sale under the belt will give a seller confidence, so they might be keener to shift something on the cheap. My advice here is that if you do go the locust route, don't be a pest – give sellers respect.

I would also avoid getting distracted by the stalls right by the entrance. Most buyers will be lured in to the sellers near the start. I like to have a quick power walk, swerve away from these people and hunt out the stalls that have all the hallmarks of containing the bread-and-butter bargains I'm after, before sniffing out the niche goods.

It's about trying to reach that five-fold profit target, and getting there early may be the best route, especially in the early days when you're a novice discovering your bread-and-butter and niche areas.

2. Try being a sloth as well

You can also be slow out of the traps and arrive at a boot sale later in the day – this is good for those weekends when you really don't want to commit to an early start. The main benefit of this is sellers are tired and more likely to accept a deal so they don't have to lug goods home. The bulk buying opportunities here are vast.

Not only will your body thank you for not having to get up at the crack of dawn, but you'll hit sellers when they are desperate, tired and will do anything not to take items back home with them.

A common misconception is that if you're not the first one in on a chilly Sunday morning, you are never going to unearth that gem. But many of the best deals I have bagged have been at the end of the day. People are too tired and lazy – they've spent all that time loading up the car, unloading and have had a day of it.

But when they are left with 20 or 30 items that they don't want to take back to their newly decluttered house, they are likely to dump it all at a charity shop. I'll often swoop in and say, 'I'll save you the trouble and take it all for a fiver.' I'm telling you, the majority of the time they'll go for it. For £5.

Does that make me a cheapskate? No, and who cares anyway? It is a clear and simple way of taking advantage of the situation. There is nothing wrong with that. It's why it is so lucrative – people are too afraid of being judged.

I have done this numerous times and then managed to make hundreds of pounds on the items I have bagged. Let's face it, most people do a car boot sale to clear their home and if they can make a bit of money while doing so, they will.

Sometimes, you might even get stuff for free, and free equals zero risk. The only danger of this tactic, however, is getting there too late and having to rush in order to meet your profit target. I recommend the sloth approach only when you have already visited a few car boot sales and know how best to navigate.

3. Common items = cheap but easy profits

The common items I search for at car boot sales and swap meets – whether in Britain, the US, France or Outer Mongolia – remain the same. I have the same key concepts and I always search for what I call my bread-and-butter items. There will always be unique stuff at these events, but there's always some key items I look for – and you should too in order to turn profits and make sure you never go broke.

One category that works well when you arrive last in the day not first, is media – CDs, DVDs, movies, video games – they can usually be found in plastic tubs on the corner of a stall. They are not a focal point item and people have no clue what to do with them.

You may be surprised by this. *Surely nobody wants these items anymore*, I can feel your confused brain telling the page. *Everything is streamed, nobody wants the clutter.* But let me tell you, it's an easy opportunity to flip profits.

We mentioned in Part I how much we love those barcode-scanning apps (see page 55) which can show the true value of these items. Now, it's impossible to look up every single CD in a box at a car boot sale so it's really about you taking a punt – and 99 times out of 100, it will work.

I wouldn't recommend spending more than 20p per item, between 3p and 10p is your sweet spot. These are such easy items to haggle on. Do sellers really want to bring home their boxes of unloved multimedia to sit around in a garage or attic?

I'll give you a prime example. I went to the Ventura, California swap meet late in the day, the very last hour, and I saw a guy who had boxes upon boxes of CDs and DVDs. He was hating life. I could see it in his face, I was getting a free read on him. I walked up to him and said, 'How much for the CDs?' He replied, 'Make me an offer.' This happens from time to time. That simple sentence opened the floodgates. There were five boxes and I didn't want to pay more than $3 a pop so I made a cheeky offer of $15, knowing the guy wanted rid. He thought about it and I expected a counter-offer of at least double. But the guy had had all his haggling superpowers drained out of him after a long day in the Californian sun, and thus accepted. I see these kind of bread-and-butter trades as such low risk. I quickly calculated there were 300 items in those boxes, meaning around five cents each.

It's so easy to scan these barcodes to receive an instant value on these items. The likelihood is that you'll at least double your money on this kind of transaction, but the hope – of course – is to find an item buried in there worth a small fortune. Like sifting through mud with a sieve for gold. It has happened to me on plenty of occasions – I've dug out a rare CD or DVD which had a limited run and it's jacked up the price and my profits.

Theoretically, my hunch was that one of the CDs or DVDs in this lot would be worth at least $15 so I would make my original stake back in a heartbeat. Worst case scenario? There were some awesome disco albums I spotted that I could listen to on the ride home – that was well worth the $15!

That gamble paid off handsomely. I made around $200 on that purchase, and *still* got to listen to *Saturday Night Fever* on my way home. But you can see how low the risk was, especially as the items were packaged nicely and the guy was well turned out, which made me believe that the goods would be in top shape. That's not always the way, but you'll get a vibe – a gut-read on a seller.

Most people also sell books at car boot sales. If you can get a heap of books, you can get a heap of profit too. Books tends to be more of a crapshoot, but if you can get them for between five and ten cents each and bulk buy them it is usually well worth the risk. At the bare minimum you'll find a book in there you'll want to read – and for the price of a regular book you'd buy in your favourite bookstore. But the majority of the time, you'll end up with at least a handful of books which will more than triple the price you paid for them.

Other bread-and-butter items for me include Converse shoes. I buy them all the time if they are under £3/$3, and I can easily sell them online for up to £30/$30. Many people hate the look of brand new trainers, they want that worn, vintage style.

Vintage tools – especially old-school, American made – are also sought after. I also keep an eye on anything that would look good in any self-respecting 'man cave'.

4. Don't bite off more than you can chew

Now, let me tell you a little story about one of my worst boot sale experiences. I was first at the gate and found this beautiful West German regulator clock. It was stunning. It was around three-and-a-half feet tall and one foot wide, with awesome Westminster chimes, the works. A classy piece of machinery.

I did everything right. Haggled hard with the seller and spent $82 on it. I knew it was a ten-bagger, worth at least $800 – if not more. So when I finally seal the deal, I walk it back to my car, full of beans, knowing I've secured a great profit. Huge smile on my face. The smile starts to wane when I realize it is heavier than I initially thought and I am struggling to get it back. Then, dear reader, I dropped it!

Smash.

I had bitten off more than I could chew. There is definitely a lesson to be learned there.

5. Beware the colourful peacock

Many sellers at these events are novices but there is one key trick some may use to entice you to a stall. Lee told me about this because he has done it himself.

Lee occasionally sells at car boot sales and says he always brings a peacock item. This is an item he has no intention of selling, but uses it to attract people to the stall where he can flog them other goods. It's a good tip to remember if you do sell at one of these meets.

At the last event he went to, his peacock item was a fancy make-up mirror, owned by his wife, that lights up. It attracted reams of female customers, who were then subsequently directed to the clothes rail to churn sales. As a buyer, these items can be distracting, and the true value can be found elsewhere on the stall. Don't get blinded by the peacock!

SUCCESSFUL TIPS FOR SELLING AT BOOT SALES

- If you do find yourself selling at a car boot sale, don't be lazy – make sure you know the true value of items.
- If you want to sell a dress, for example, for £5, price it at £7. You can then haggle down to that £5 price point.
- It may sound basic, but make sure you clean the items you're selling – and display everything, don't hide it away in boxes.
- I encourage bundle pricing on items you know not to be worth much. This includes multimedia, the items that you've already seen are worth peanuts on those barcode apps and are willing to accept offers. Remember, you already have prices for all the goods on your stall and are trying to trick buyers to part with more cash for them than you know them to be worth.
- So what if someone really lowballs you? As a seller, there is one magic word: no. It's okay to say no – don't feel embarrassed when someone gives you an offer. If someone uses the *Pawn Stars* technique against you – there is damage, the item's not in pristine condition – go along with it. Say you know, you've noticed that, and that's why the price is what it is. If you're not happy with the price, just say no, even if they are persistent.

- Make sure you bring all those plastic bags you've been hoarding to make life easier for your buyers.
- Get plenty of change before you turn up, otherwise you have the potential to miss sales.

CAR BOOT SALE 'APPS'

It's worth pointing out, in the digital age, that there are various marketplaces in which you can buy and sell goods online – but the chances of finding a bargain on them are slim to none.

Plenty of people sell on apps such as Facebook, Gumtree and Shpock, and it can be a good way to sell certain items, such women's fashion or old bikes, especially if you have good photography and lighting skills.

It is quite easy to find designer brands at charity shops and car boot sales, for example, clean them up and flip them for a profit on these apps, especially if you can make them look good in photographs. This is quite a good niche to carve out and is worth considering. But we still believe that turning up physically at car boot events is a better tactic.

USING THE BLUEPRINT: CAR BOOT SALES

Car boot sales should be your 'second to last' resort for selling (see page 34). On the flipside, as a buyer you should expect most sellers to be thinking this way as well. Car boot sales are the grassroots – literally – a ground floor opportunity for you to start finding your niche. Wake up at your own pace, learn at your own pace and haggle at your own pace. Car boot sales are fun – enjoy them!

- Find a bread-and-butter item such as multimedia to target at these events to make small profits.
- Find a few niche areas such as boomboxes or cameras to spot to make bigger profits.
- Trust your gut on an item. Glean as much information as you can about it, walk away, research on your phone then make a decision.
- Be first at the car boot sales, head to the back and make low offers to snag items on the cheap to reach your five-fold profit target – ideal for newbies.
- Or be last and take advantage of those not wanting to take items home – better when you're more experienced and need less time.
- Multimedia: try to work out a price per item in those boxes people want to be rid of – they can be flipped for a nice profit.
- Get a read on a seller. Body language will suggest haggling opportunities and potentially the condition of items you're buying.
- Have other bread-and-butter buy targets too – as well as multimedia and books, I look for Converse trainers and American-made tools.
- When discovering your niche, building knowledge will make you an expert quickly – but don't pick too many niches and expect the occasional disappointment.
- Bulk buying multimedia and clothes can work well at boot sales, if you can get a rock bottom price and know how and where you're going to resell.

- Have a plan with the items you buy. If they are cumbersome, it is likely you'll need help getting them back to the car!
- Haggle properly. If you don't ask, you don't get – you'll never see the seller again, so why worry?
- Don't be afraid to walk away – don't get too emotionally attached to items you're looking to buy. Take your time.
- Beware peacock items. Many sellers know the tricks of the trade and will bring an item or two that'll dazzle you into coming to their stand.
- Selling at a car boot? Make sure you have maxed out the profit potential elsewhere and bring your own peacock!
- Car boot apps and websites are good, but turning up to physical events can be more rewarding (and fun!).

RESOURCES

Car Boot Junction (www.carbootjunction.com) – a comprehensive list of car boot sales taking place across the country.

LESSON 12: CHARITY SHOPS AND THRIFT STORES – GET STUCK IN!

LEVEL: Beginner
PROFIT POTENTIAL: ££

Charity shops can be untapped treasure troves of wares to snap up and sell on for a profit. Don't ever feel bad about doing this. If you do find the Holy Grail, a hundred-bagger, remember: the charity shop was donated the item to sell, you're doing it a favour by buying it to clear more space for other items to be stocked and to keep their revenue flowing in.

If you're still feeling bad, you can always donate some of your hard-gotten gains later down the line. If I find a real score in a charity shop, I donate some excess inventory to that same shop so they can benefit as well. As I always say, it's a win-win in the circle of resale life.

Also included in this lesson are 'thrift stores'. These are resale stores that have got a little trendier in recent years. If you're ever holidaying in the US, these can be worth visiting – they often have a number of easy buys to bring home for resale, potentially paying for your trip.

WHAT IS IT? THE ESSENTIALS

There are more than 11,000 charity shops in Britain. That is an incredible amount. Many generous people donate goods they no longer want in their home, while feeling good about doing so in the process. There are excellent charity shops, good charity shops – and ones that you're unlikely to ever snag a bargain at.

Essentially, the lovely volunteers at these shops go through all of the bags they are donated, and largely sift out the bad stuff. That, in a way, makes this an easier sideline than the car boot sale. The more high-end an area – think affluent towns and parts of cities – the higher the stakes. In other words, rich folk are likely to hand over designer items to these shops. Thrift stores are essentially 'upmarket' charity shops. These can also have bargains, but tend to be more common in the US than the UK.

Many people see charity shop openings as a sort of decay of the British high street. That is, other shops have closed and charity shops have moved in, along with coffee shops and what feels like an endless number of betting shops. According to NGO Finance, in 1990 there were around 3,000 UK charity shops. This doubled by 2000 and has since roughly doubled again.

The most profitable, Statista data shows, are – in order: British Heart Foundation, Oxfam, Cancer Research UK, Barnado's, Sue Ryder, Salvation Army, Age UK, British Red Cross, Scope and Marie Curie. Rather incredibly, it is thought that Oxfam is the largest retailer of secondhand books in Europe, selling more than 10 million a year.

Charity shops are usually staffed by unpaid volunteers, with a shop manager who does earn a salary. Around nine in ten items in a charity shop are from donations, although some shops have their own lines of new items. The concept is thought to have started in the late 19th century in Wolverhampton, on the outskirts of Birmingham, by a charity raising funds for the blind.

It was during the Second World War that charity shops became more widespread as people looked to raise money for the war effort. The Red Cross opened its first charity shop in Bond Street in this era and, during the war, around 350 new shops were opened – some permanent, some temporary. The shop licence required that all goods on offer were gifts – they were not allowed to purchase items to sell on in the shop.

It is believed that each charity shop saves 40 tonnes of textiles every year by selling them in the shop or selling them to textile merchants to recycle or reuse.

ACTION POINT: Check on Google Maps. How many charity shops are there in a 15-mile radius of your home? How many could you potentially visit in a day? Get it in the calendar.

WHY IT'S WORTH YOUR TIME

Charity shops can often have untapped gems, and many people pass them up simply because they do not want to step foot inside. It's their loss, we think these shops are great.

One benefit of looking in a charity shop, opposed to a car boot sale or antiques market, is simply that the shops tend to be fairly small, giving you an easier chance to sniff out bargains. They also tend to be laid out fairly simply – a clothes section, a book section, a multimedia section, a jigsaw section…

It can be best to visit these shops early on a week day, when they're not as busy but new stock has been put out. There are a number of tips and tricks we're about to outline to maximize profits from your time.

PROFIT POTENTIAL

Charity shops offer an untapped ceiling for profits. It's easy to pick up designer clothes, for example, that are priced fairly and you know you can double or triple your money simply by listing them online.

For example, a handbag bought in Oxfam in Kingston a decade ago for £20 turned out to be a piece of art by haute couture milliner Philip Treacy, who confirmed it was a rare Andy Warhol Elvis print, with only ten ever being made. It attracted bids north of £300,000.

Meanwhile, in a charity shop in North Carolina, someone paid $2.48 for what he thought was a reproduction copy of the US Declaration of Independence. Yellowing and rolled up, it transpired to be one of 20 official copies commissioned by President John Quincy Adams – and sold for $477,650.

These prove that charity shops can be a good stomping ground, so don't be afraid to get involved. Don't expect huge wins like that, but you should be able to bag a shed load of bread-and-butter buys, with the odd niche purchase to turn profits.

Don't forget you can use the barcode trick in charity shops. That is, you can use those barcode-scanning apps we mentioned earlier to see if you can make money. We'll reiterate: you are doing the charity shop a favour by buying an item for the asking price and giving them more space to sell more goods.

HOW TO FIND A GOOD CHARITY SHOP

Charity shops are similar to antique shops in the fact that you never know what you will find – there's always something new. Goods aren't cherry picked by the charity shop employees, they get what they get and then they just put it out. I don't think of it in terms of choosing a good shop, rather using my time effectively.

I like to look at it in terms of the concentration of charity shops and head somewhere I can visit several at the same time. At least I know I can hit five in one go, as opposed to one that may have had quality stuff in the past.

As previously mentioned, try to visit shops in affluent areas where the quality of donated goods will be high – you just might bag those designer goods at a snip.

Tips and tricks for success

Spending a day going to charity shops and thrift stores is literally searching in the rough – no disrespect to charity shops. It's simply trying to find those few hidden gems.

It can go a multitude of ways because you never know what you're going to find. There's many different ways you can go about it. The skill set that we're going to use here can be used in a number of situations.

I. Hunt for multimedia first

Multimedia is one of the most profitable things that I sell from charity shops because of the convenience of being able to get instantaneous resale values on items while you're standing in the shop. It can seem a little tacky going around scanning every single book to look up prices on your phone, while a volunteer behind the counter is staring at you wondering what you are doing. Are you trying to steal all my stuff? However, it's easy to find media worth, say, £3 priced at 50p – that's six times your money.

The chance of making serious money from charity shops is rare – the most effective use of your time when you walk into a charity shop is to focus on those £2, £3 and even £1 profit margins and go for volume, rather than going on a wild goose chase to try to find one diamond, one gemstone, that could potentially not be there at all.

So concentrate on those easy pickings you know will be there. There's the exact same bookshelf in every single charity shop up and down the country – kids' books on top, big bulky nonsense books on the bottom and DVDs, CDs and a few cassette tapes in between.

2. Ask yourself how much is filtered

Most charity shops like to filter their donations to pick out valuable items to be sold elsewhere for a bigger profit. However, at certain times of the year, charity shops can be swamped with items from household clear outs and the amount of time volunteers get to sort through the bags is limited. Unlike the antiques experts we talk about in the next lesson, these volunteers don't always filter out the valuable items because they don't have the knowledge or time to do it.

If I was employed at a charity shop, I would be able to filter out what's worth money and what's not worth money to maximize the profits of the shop but some volunteers won't be so good at it as others.

The number one thrift store in the US is Goodwill. This not-for-profit organization takes billions of dollars of revenue each year for charity and has its own auction sites. This means there are more skilled people filtering through the items as they come in to designate exactly where they go for resale. They have the choice of selling items at a high-end auction site or staying in the local shop.

Britain is scattered with larger 'chain' shops, such as the British Heart Foundation and Oxfam – which may be more professional in their approach and have more staff – but also smaller charity shops benefitting local charities.

I see 'volunteers wanted' signs in the window as a good indication that the charity shop may be a little short on staff, and that could mean less filtering and more goodies on offer. I'll say this again: you may be taking advantage, but you are also helping clear the shop of stock so more can go in.

I also gain this information by overhearing employees talking. If I hear them say they are volunteers (rather than paid staff) or that they are fulfilling their community service by working in the shop, it makes me think that I'm glad this charity shop is giving opportunities to people who are seeking them, but also that they're not investing time to find people who understand that certain items have certain price points in terms of value.

3. Start with the winter coats

I've already mentioned that the more salubrious an area you're in, the more likely there is to be designer goods on offer in charity shops – including clothes. However, you want to be efficient with your time and digging through clothes is one of the most time-consuming things you could possibly do if you don't know exactly what you're after. Looking at tags on every single item is going to be difficult.

Nearly 80 per cent of a charity shop's stock is likely to be clothes – so do we just immediately write off four-fifths of its inventory? No, not necessarily – but you must understand it can be time consuming, not just rifling through old clothes, but cleaning them up and photographing them well if you are selling online.

But there are simple tricks to use to turn quick profits. A simple framework I use is this: If I'm looking at a clothing rack I know that – designer items aside – a winter coat will usually be more valuable than a t-shirt and they're an easy spot. If I were to look at a clothing rack six feet away, I could spot a winter jacket but not a t-shirt and its brand.

I tend to focus first on looking at the jackets and coats, knowing I can grab them without having to dig through every shirt, blouse and dress in the shop. And I know my way round all of these items as I have a vintage clothes store.

Having a flick through thick jackets is likely to be way more worth your time – and it's easy to spot, say, a Carhartt over a Primark one. You will spot visual nuances just doing a quick flip through.

Sometimes, though, it's not just about the profit. I can't count the number of times I've been looking for a resale score and ended up replacing my old jacket for one I've found. Sometimes, you need to savour your finds and enjoy them for yourself rather than just thinking about the money.

4. Move on to other clothes

Once you master those quick jacket wins, level two is digging through t-shirts. Vintage tour t-shirts are incredibly hot right now, as are brands synonymous with the 1990s and unusual sports clothing.

Band t-shirts are usually easy to spot as they tend to be quite busy in design – and the majority of the time, they'll show a year and locations the band played. Anything pre-2000 is selling like hot cakes right now, from metal bands to the Spice Girls. Posh Spice and the gang are still highly desirable.

You can always be on the lookout for these if you're digging through t-shirts and, in a future lesson, I will lift the lid on a huge win I had from doing this.

ACTION POINT: Look up a tour shirt of your favourite band and see how much it is selling for, depending on the year and tour.

---

5. Find off-season buys

On the winter jacket theme, although I'm not a huge fan of holding inventory – I like to buy items to sell on almost straight away as storage generally consumes money and goes against my profit margin it can sometimes pay to take advantage of seasonal differences.

Winter jackets are likely to be priced cheaper as summer begins, before September rolls around and the prices nudge up again when people need them more. And the charity shop will want rid of winter jackets in the summer months as they take up valuable space.

Storing a dozen good winter jackets, ready to unleash once autumn begins, can boost profits. When you're buying winter clothes out of season, you're immediately eliminating competition from the end consumer.

6. Remember to build contacts

It's always worth getting friendly with staff in a charity shop, asking employees to tell you when the best new stuff comes in or whether they've got any weird stuff that isn't yet out on display. It's a 50-50 shot. Some volunteers will say that if it's not on the shop floor, I can't sell it. But occasionally, if you get friendly enough, they might invite you in the back to see if you can find anything good. It can be great having the first crack, whether it's junk or not.

You could also strike a deal, potentially, to offer to donate a certain percentage of any resale profit you make back to the shop. Maybe 25 per cent – or whatever figure you choose – back to the charity. That would be for you to decide.

These charity shops want money. They might have the most valuable antiques in their shops, but that's not going to help cover their expenses and help raise money for their charity. Really, that valuable item is worth nothing to them.

It could be worth building contacts at a few different charity shops.

7. Rinse and repeat

Another way to build these bridges is to become a point of contact for certain items that come in to a charity shop. I've done this in the past – asked a volunteer to call me if video games, a certain genre of movie or textbooks come in. This, again, is win-win. The charity shop has a guaranteed sale to remove stock, and I know I can buy these items to flip into a neat profit.

What you're doing is conveying information to the charity based on either your personal tastes or your previous sales experience. If you've sold these movies, games, textbooks or whatever it may be in the past, use that knowledge to rinse and repeat. You want to make things as simple as possible and save time, knowing that someone in the charity shop is essentially doing the digging for you.

You're saving time so you can focus on a new project or something different – it's establishing a passive income, because the only thing you have to do is pick up the items and pay for them, rather than spending an extra half hour digging.

If you can cut your time in half now, you are mitigating and lowering your risk, and also lowering the time and effort needed to get this stuff to potentially turn a profit.

8. Look for a boombox niche here too

I talked about finding a boombox niche at car boot sales – and while the majority of items on sale at charity shops are clothes and multimedia (and puzzles without all the pieces), there can be the occasional diamond, emerald, or ruby in the rough. But it might not be where you think it is until you get that experience and amass the information I keep mentioning.

You are already in the charity shop, so it's worth casting your eye around for glassware and porcelain, for example – it's good to learn passively about these types of items, and focus on particular manufacturers. Then you can start establishing whether it is worth buying that brand or it isn't, so you can be well versed.

People are always fixated on finding that one cheap item they can sell for a huge profit. What I'm saying is focus on bulk buying items that you can sell for small profits and, occasionally, you might pick up a profitable item like this.

Let me give an example. One item I have hoarded for a long time is 1980s boomboxes, as mentioned previously. If you go on eBay and search the sold prices for vintage boomboxes, it will blow your mind.

That aside, computers that are five to ten years old are not generally worth much – unless they have scrap value inside – but those older than that can be valuable. Imagine how many have ended up in landfill – they are becoming extinct. Think pre-laptop, smartphone, tablet – these are computing dinosaurs.

I have never found an original Apple computer, which can sell for big bucks, but I bought one of the first IBM computers, the 5150 – it weighed about 80 pounds. It was a massive thing of the sort you see in 1980s financial movies, like *Wall Street* – guys with slicked-back hair, pinstripe suits and behemoths of computers. I bought it for $5 and I sold it to a collector for $600. I did this after finding another 5150 at a house clearance and selling it on, as mentioned earlier in the book

There's plenty of money to be made and it's a relatively untapped market, as most buyers worry that it won't work and will need repair work, which could be difficult or costly. It's worth bearing in mind that there's enough people out there able to repair these items so it's more important to check that they have the original components, rather than whether they work or not.

Another example is radio tubes, which I mentioned earlier. They're not made anymore – whatever is out there is all there'll ever be so it drives up the price. Nintendo doesn't make the N64 anymore. People pine after them, want one, and as more and more disappear from the earth and end up in landfill, the more the price drives up, especially if you can find one in its original box.

SHOULD YOU HAGGLE AT A CHARITY SHOP?

Charity shops have a positive impact on society – let's not take away from the good they do. But on the flip side, let's not apologize for the fact that you're trying to get the best bang for your buck. I would say that the decision to haggle or not should come down to the volume you are buying – if you're spending more than £100, say, I think you have more arsenal to do it.

It could be worth making an offer for an entire shelf of books, games or media. At some price it will be worth the charity shop getting rid of a whole load of stock rather than spending the time and effort involved in counting and scanning every single book. Use your own discretion. But also be aware that the charity shop is there to make money for a good cause – we want to make it a win-win for everyone.

USING THE BLUEPRINT: CHARITY SHOPS

The number of charity shops out there is immense, the staff tend to be friendly and there is a real range of decent buys to be had. Try to hit as many as you can in one swoop to maximize your transportation costs and don't be afraid to get stuck in.

We'll say it once more: these items have been donated and it is a win-win for all involved if you buy from these shops, whatever profit you make on the items. The charity selling will be receiving your cash and freeing up space for more stock.

- Scan those barcodes – books, CDs and DVDs can help produce small gains. They'll be your staple bread-and-butter resale buys.
- Yes, staff do filter items that are donated, but they can be swamped with household clear outs so there could be bargains to snaffle.

- Remember your niche – charity shops are crammed full of clothes, so focus on one area such as winter jackets to build big profits.
- Keep your eyes skimmed for quick clothing wins, such as band t-shirts.
- If you can buy off-season items at cheap prices, you may be able to hold onto them and sell at the opportune moment. Remember those trends and patterns we talked about in Part II.
- It is worth building contacts at charity shops. They could be able to tell you when stuff is arriving or when a certain item comes in, if you build a rapport with them.
- There are other niches to carve out besides clothes, such as electronics, which many other people won't want to touch.
- Yes, you can haggle in a charity shop but we wouldn't do it on individual items unless they're priced very high.

LESSON 13: ANTIQUES CENTRES, RETRO AND VINTAGE STORES – KNOWLEDGE IS POWER

LEVEL: Intermediate
PROFIT POTENTIAL: ££££

Wherever I am in the world, I love a good antiques market and I think Britain has some of the best – they are dotted everywhere and I find many of the towns and villages in which they are located rather charming. My parents own an antiques mall in Los Angeles and whenever I'm back, I pitch in. I love it. I am constantly learning, picking up new ideas and tricks – no two days are the same.

Antiques may conjure up images of sweeping country manors and bespectacled gentlemen in tweed jackets thumbing vases, but let's bust that myth right now. These days, they are highly popular with a younger, latte-sipping crowd, looking for unusual items for their homes.

I think much of the misconception about these types of places comes from television shows, where often well-spoken antiques buyers chase after the same thing, and do some haggling with a seller who they usually already know. The items then go under the hammer later in the show, usually don't make a profit, and it all gets a bit sad.

When it comes to buying and selling at these places, I want you to get that image out of your mind.

WHAT IS IT? THE ESSENTIALS

Antiques shops and centres are essentially locations in which you can find items for sale that are relatively old – but not always – and are rare or unique.

Technically, to be an antique, an item should be more than a 100 years old, but these centres and shops usually stock all sorts of bric-a-brac. Some will specialize in certain areas, such as furniture or lighting, others will be more general.

The quality of items varies, from extremely high-quality expensive goods – typically seen in affluent areas – to very low-quality cheaper items, usually found in less affluent places. The high-end places are unlikely to be of interest to us – we're looking for places that are mid-range to low.

Lee's favourite, as previously mentioned, is Battlesbridge Antiques Centre in Essex, which has 80 dealers in a variety of shops, selling all sorts of goods. It's one of his favourite ways to pass a Sunday afternoon.

The UK is dotted with these places. Petworth in West Sussex has more than 30 antiques shops; Honiton in Devon has nearly 100 dealers in over a dozen locations; Perth in Scotland has an abundance of shops and centres; Hay-on-Wye is a good option in Wales; and Enniskillen, Northern Ireland, is too. And, if you don't end up finding a big win, you're sure to enjoy a jolly good spot of perusing and people watching.

It can be worth visiting these places in the UK, but also in Europe and the US too, if you're visiting, with the aim of paying for your trip by buying and selling some items you find.

Retro and vintage stores are also included in this lesson. They may not technically sell antiques – although it depends on your definition – but the principles are the same.

WHY IT'S WORTH YOUR TIME

Antiques shops do often contain overpriced items. I can say that as someone who has been on both sides of this antiques shop coin, both selling and buying. Let's face it, most of the goods on offer have been bought to sell on with profit in mind, which is exactly what you are also trying to do. The profit has been sucked out of them already.

But that said, there are still ways to turn these visits into a profit. You need to look out for telltale signs that a place is worth entering and, as mentioned elsewhere in this book, build your visits into your day, week, month or year and pop in when you happen to be passing to be efficient with your precious time.

PROFIT POTENTIAL

I have turned over roughly $3 million of antiques sales in the last decade, largely by buying items and selling them on in my parents' antiques shop or by other methods.

The profit potential in these places may have been used up to some extent because the dealers have sucked the profit pig teat a little already, but that doesn't mean there aren't deals to be had and treasure to be found.

HOW TO FIND A GOOD ANTIQUES CENTRE, RETRO OR VINTAGE STORE

Antiques centres are essentially fancy thrift stores or indoor car boot sales. They cater to people who have no interest in going out in the freezing cold at 6am to a car boot sale to try to find an antique in a pile of trash and rubbish. They are filtered versions of the boot sale and thrift store. Prices tend to be higher because of this and the work that goes into finding good items and the rental overheads. Some people simply don't like digging and are prepared to pay more for items to avoid it.

Antiques centres are a conglomerate of different people who classify themselves as antiques dealers. Now, an antiques dealer sounds fancy, but just like any industry, there are many good antiques dealers, and there are plenty of bad antiques dealers. You don't need any sort of proper qualifications or accreditation. With secondhand goods, as long as you have the money to pay the rent, you're pretty much free to call yourself whatever you like.

The key to visiting antiques centres is not about finding certain items, it's about finding value – whether you're at your local centre or somewhere new. The perception is that every item in an antiques centre is good. You never know what you're going to find which is exciting. But these items have already been filtered, researched…and they've already been priced. Finding a million-pound item in an antiques centre does happen on rare occasions, but less often than at a car boot sale.

Before you step in the door, remember that you're hunting for value. One way to do this is noticing the specific circumstances of the individual dealers. Let's say you're in a big antiques centre with 100 dealers. They have 100 different sets of expertise and, potentially, 100 different sets of circumstances.

You can have a dealer who is brand new, still trying to figure values out. Often their prices are super-high or super-low – you'll want to take advantage of the latter.

You'll also want to look out for the people at the end of their career. Antiques, by their nature, tend to be catered towards the older generation. So when your customers are in this age range, it makes sense that the dealer themselves might also be. You want to look for those people who are going into antiques retirement, if you will, trying to liquidate their items so they can leave and not be stuck with a bunch of different stuff.

You want to fixate your eyes on two different colours – yellow and red – generally used for sale tags. Look for those colours and any telltale keywords – 'sale', 'clearance', 'going out of business', whatever it may be. That's what to look for when choosing antiques centres to visit.

Also, make sure you Google properly. The majority of these

establishments have reviews so see how they're rated. Some will have five stars because they're nice and clean, well kept, the employees are nice, the items are good, and so forth. Others might have a low rating because they are grimy, the people are jerks – but the items may be excellent. You have to decipher: is this worth my time?

The way I often decide whether to visit is simply based on volume. If I know that one antiques centre has 300 dealers, while another has only 10 dealers, I'm more likely to visit the first to make best use of my time. That's not to say that the smaller one isn't as good a potential opportunity, but for the sake of your time, and the likelihood of finding a deal, it's more advantageous to go to the larger one and then work your way backwards.

WHAT IS AN 'ANTIQUE'?

The word 'antique' is a bit arbitrary to me. I prefer to look at an item's style. But I would say anything made up until just after the Second World War could be called an antique now. In 60 years' time, 1980s items – my childhood toys – are going to be 'antiques'. An antique Teenage Mutant Ninja Turtle action figure? What the heck does that even mean?

I would call toys and clothes from the 1980s 'retro' or 'vintage' rather than 'antique'. There's an era difference. I also think of 1950s and 1960s items – your ice-cream parlour, Elvis Presley style – as more 'vintage' in my mind.

Items from the 90s, and soon the early 2000s, I think of these items in terms of era, rather than as 'antiques'. Basically, 'antique' is just a word like 'rich' or 'poor' – you decide what it means to you.

Tips and tricks for success

1. Learn the art of the antiques haggle

Don't be intimidated by the words 'fine art,' 'luxury' or other sexy adjectives used to describe antiques stores. Treat them like fancy indoor car boot sales. Don't disrespect the business owners or its patrons, but don't feel any different asking for a deal just like you would any other resale opportunity. The worst they can do is say no, just in a fancier outfit.

The unwritten rule is that these places give discounts if you ask. But you must instigate it. Items are priced with haggling in mind. That said, you need to be a little bit more highbrow than at your local car boot sale. It's a bit tacky to go into an antiques centre and say, 'Will you take £10 for this £30 item?'. At a boot sale it's a free for all and it's more encouraged.

When you ask for a discount don't reveal what you're willing to pay. For example, don't ask if they will take £50 off, ask what their best price is. Many times, they'll go much lower than the amount you're thinking. Don't cut yourself short – remember, I am frequently on both sides of the coin. Let the seller state their discount and justify the reason why, and then go from there in terms of trying to get the best price possible – you'll be surprised.

If you are interested in a high-value item, haggling is especially worthwhile, particularly on items above £500. Your discount could be hundreds of pounds, which all goes into your potential profit margin.

You could also try taking the item you want to the seller while covering the price tag – especially if you know it's been in the shop for a while. Let's say an item has been there for 18 months, priced at £100. The seller might not know how much they initially valued it at, and may say £70 when you ask the price. You can then haggle from there.

That doesn't always work, but it can be worth a shot.

The seller establishes the starting price, you go lower. It doesn't matter what the number is – go back to our haggling advice in Lesson 7 (see page 124) for a refresher.

Antiques shops need to sell a certain number of items in a day, a week, a month to get new stock in. They need a turnaround. They also need to make sales to pay the rent. You should go into these places with that mind, knowing that they need to pay their bills. It can also be worth a visit at the end of the month, when rent is likely to be due.

Buying multiple items in an antiques centre can also lead to good discounts. If multiple items present themselves as potential value and opportunity to make some money, haggle. Generally, when I walk into an antiques mall, I take a quick walk through and if there are any treasures there I ask, 'If I spend between $500 and $1,000, what kind of discounts can I get?'. This immediately opens the door to opportunity as they see I'm willing to open my wallet, but this is more of a pro tip as your resale game grows and evolves.

Remember: don't make antiques haggling emotional. You'll just end up a sideshow character on a short-lived American reality show about storage auctions.

ACTION POINT: Haggle at home in the mirror, pretending to speak to someone you've met in your life who has been difficult to talk to. When you're ready, have the confidence to go into an antiques store and show off your new skills. Revel in any discount you can get.

---

2. Find the low-hanging fruit

The first thing I look for in an antiques centre or vintage shop is what I call the low-hanging fruit: the easy wins. I look for those deviations in the stock that nobody's offering any money on because the client base isn't in the area the shop's in. But if I buy it and take it elsewhere to sell, I'll be able to turn a profit simply because my potential customer base will be exponentially larger. You want to have that secret knowledge and use it to your advantage.

If I'm in an affluent area, I'm instantly drawn to rusty gold and items that may be of interest to the common person, those I dub 'man-cave pieces'. These generally fall into the following categories: Breweriana (alcohol-related items), vintage advertising signs and merchandise, automobilia, electronics, music memorabilia and Americana. Old-school beer taps are cool, but are wealthy antiques collectors going to be decorating their multi-million pound homes with them? Or original Oasis tour posters? 1950s Coca-Cola porcelain signs? Highly doubtful.

If I'm in a working-class area, I'll look for high-end items like French provincial furniture, as they are unlikely to fit in terraced homes and they take up plenty of space on a shop floor, so the owners will want rid.

This was a concept I had on my television show *British Treasure, American Gold*. I was buying items from Britain and taking them over to Los Angeles, where a bigger client base was waiting. These were items buyers may never have seen in the US before. My aim was to find unique and high-dollar items no local dealers could offer.

Bringing back items to LA from Britain justified the price going up, simply because no one there had seen these things before and they were willing to pay any price. You can apply this principle to the North and South of Britain, West and East, parts of Europe, and the internet where the entire world can potentially be your buyer. Offering something unique can drive up the price in certain areas.

A great example of this is bringing items involving Princess Diana to the US where buyers go wild for unique Royal Family memorabilia in good condition. It's worth bearing this in mind if you visit the US for a holiday and want to sell a couple of items from your hand luggage, and vice versa, as I'll explain shortly.

ONE HUNDRED GREEN BOTTLES, SITTING IN A ROW

This is one of the prime examples of when I made a tonne of money by buying in an antiques centre. It also highlights how 30 seconds of homework would have made the dealer that same profit.

You may remember that old playground song – you know the one – where you count down ten green bottles, sitting in a row. I don't, because we didn't have it in the US, but Lee reliably informs me it was sung to relieve boredom. It goes:

Ten green bottles hanging on the wall,
Ten green bottles hanging on the wall.
And if one green bottle should accidentally fall,
There'll be nine green bottles hanging on the wall.
So on and so forth. God, you Brits can be a little weird.

Anyway, take those ten green bottles and multiply them by ten – and I'll tell you about one of the best scores of my resale career.

It was via an antiques dealer, not some poor person in the street. He had owned his shop for more than three decades and it delivered what I call the Holy Grail – a hundred-bagger – that's buying something and making a hundred times your money on it. Yes, you read that right, a hundred times.

He had these green bottles in a fruit box – around a hundred of them. He was tired of moving them from one shelf to the next and didn't feel like cleaning them. They were weird and awkward, and clearly were being shown no love by buyers entering the shop.

They were a hexagonal shape, pretty small and dirty inside. They were not visually appealing and, for that reason, he wasn't shifting them. Also, being glass, they were incredibly difficult to sell online – they were brittle and you'd have to wrap them well in order for them to survive the journey to the buyer. He would need ten rolls of bubble wrap just to have a chance of them arriving safely.

I knew all this and played it to my advantage. I made an offer: I'd take all hundred off him for a tenner. I had a gut instinct that I'd be able to sell them for at least £1 each, so I'd make a profit no matter what.

After a little research, it transpired these bottles were 1890s apothecary bottles, worth around £10 each. I sold them to a speciality guy who deals only in antique medicine bottles. I made nearly £1,000 in profit.

Now, it wasn't as easy as it sounds. I was in the bathroom all week in my rubber gloves washing those bottles to make them look nearly new. But, entering that antiques shop and understanding the potential pay-off was worth my time. I knew old bottles can be highly collectible and I wasn't going to be lazy for the sake of losing a couple of quid.

In reality, you need to do the maths to see if it is worth your time. If you can turn an £8 buy into a £10 sell and you have a hundred of that item, it can add up real quick. If you can clean each item up in, say, 30 seconds to make that £2, you are essentially earning £240 an hour.

3. Know what to spot

Recently, I went into an antiques centre. On the fourth floor, in the back corner, was a dealer who was having a sale and was clearly struggling. It was common sense – this person had the worst spot in the entire centre. But the quality of the goods was so good. There were nice porcelain signs, antique radios and other vintage equipment – the items had that man-cave vibe.

I asked an employee – who turned out to be the manager – if they were willing to sell all the contents of their booth. I did a deal with them and way underpaid for everything that I got. I believe the enormity of that opportunity was too tempting and offered the owner a complete way out of the business.

These upfront opportunities come few and far between and you have to recognize them when they come. I took home every single item that person had – an extreme version of taking advantage – but keep an eye out for opportunities on a smaller scale.

4. Recognize your dealer

There are two different kinds of dealers. The first are the hardcore guys that have been doing it their entire lives. They have the knowledge of every single thing they have. Unless you're a collector that wants that specific item, I would try to avoid these dealers as best as you can as you won't make a profit from them.

Then there are the hobbyists. Dealing is their version of being in a sports team and having fun. It's more important to them than tracking prices online and getting the best price they can from their customers.

If you identify that half of antiques dealers are just people who enjoy the fun of collecting, buying and selling like so many of us, it isn't as scary when you go in their shop. Not everyone is from *Dickinson's Real Deal* – those guys in bowties looking to take you to the cleaners.

Don't be intimidated by anyone in this business, myself included. No matter how many bowties, TV shows or snobby attitudes we have, we are just people who are looking to make money buying and selling stuff. You can do this too and don't let anyone else tell you otherwise.

5. Hunt those nooks and crannies

Some antiques centres can be a real maze, with hundreds of dealers and floor after floor of goods. They are often pretty uninspiring places – they have pockets, nooks and crannies that have been untouched for quite some time. It can be worth finding the spots other buyers might not reach or, if they do, they are fatigued by the time they get there. All it takes to explore is a mini dig.

Often you'll find items that have been there for years, gathering dust. These are golden items to haggle hard on, if you spot something good that other eyes haven't. You can play this to your advantage – these items have clearly been there for a long time, they either want your money or they don't. Just remember, though, some dealers are incredibly stubborn and that might be the reason why those items are still there.

Here's an example: precious metal. The price of silver and gold has fluctuated in the last decade. Gold, at time of writing, is at an all-time high. If you look outside the obvious – jewellery – you could find, say, an old sterling silver ice scoop or dining set priced five years ago at £30 a gram which, today, is worth £45 a gram. It hasn't been re-priced accordingly.

This is actually a common household insurance mistake, Lee tells me. If you are burgled but haven't had your jewellery valued for a decade, you might end up being short-changed, because your gold, silver or diamonds have probably gone up in value. You're still paying for insurance cover at the original price.

You want to look for those little nuggets in the nooks and crannies of antiques shops and do some digging. Earlier I mentioned those dusty old apothecary bottles. I should also add to that story that when I noticed them in that old box, some were broken and they were all dusty and unloved. The key was asking the dealer without touching them, as I wanted them to continue to look sad. Twelve bottles had shattered, but I saved a hundred of them.

6. Look for vintage band t-shirts

One of the best items I've ever bought at an antiques mall actually ended up being a little frustrating as it was right under my nose.

I was looking to snap up clothes for the vintage clothing store I run with my wife Nicole. We go on these little travel adventures, stopping at thrift stores and swap meets to find fashion gems as we spend time together and get to see some of the States.

On one such trip, after a few days hopping and skipping, we'd done fairly well but hadn't found any real 'big' hitters. On the way home, we stopped off at my family's antiques mall and had a look at what was on offer in a vintage clothing shop there. We scooped up one band tour t-shirt from the 1980s, then another, then another. Before we knew it, we had five of them.

From a vintage clothes perspective, this is like the Holy Grail – depending on the bands. These were Queen, Van Halen and ZZ Top. We thought they were going to be expensive. They were priced at $5 each – or $25 for the lot. They ended up being worth a touch over $1,800.

The moral of the story: band tees, as we've already mentioned, are highly sought after at the moment, and can be worth a mint if rare enough. And just because they're in a vintage clothing store doesn't mean the owner knows their worth.

Wherever you're going, it's worth popping your head into a few antiques shops on the way so you're not making a special trip. But don't overlook your local area too. We were ecstatic with that score, but also a little upset that we'd travelled nearly 1,000 miles to find items that were a few miles from home.

HOW TO PAY FOR YOUR FLIGHT TO THE US

The secret to paying for your holiday while on holiday? Take an empty case. I challenge you to try to pay – or at least partly pay – for a trip to the US by bringing an empty case and filling it up with clothes or other items. When you bring them back to the UK, they become unique items, and people like to try to be individuals.

Let's say you come back with 30 t-shirts that you've paid a dollar apiece for. These could be a mix of band t-shirts, location t-shirts, t-shirts with US sports emblazoned on them, which are bang on trend at the moment, US apparel clothing and whatever else you can get your mitts on easily at a flea market or thrift store.

Let's now say you can sell them for £8–£10 a pop for 25 of them, and you manage to unearth five that you can list for a bit more, say £15. You're looking at a £325 return, minus the small outlay and the cost, potentially, of taking that extra case.

Believe me, this is easily done. When you list the clothes in the UK, you can say that they're from the US and are unlikely to be found anywhere else. It ramps up the price.

It's not just clothing either. You may be able to find some of your niche items in these places too. I'm surprised more travellers don't take advantage of this. You can pay for a holiday pretty quickly with resale.

STAR WARS: GRAVITY-DEFYING PROFITS

One of my best retro buys were 12 original *Star Wars* action figures in their retail packaging. I didn't just buy them because I am a nerd (I mean, I am), I bought them because I already had a buyer in mind from previous sales.

Because I was spending a vast amount of money – £800 – I was wary of the risk but I purchased them with two things in mind. One: I had the confidence that I could sell them on rather quickly, or at least some of them. If I knew someone who would buy four of them, for example, I could take this chunk out of my purchase price and reduce the risk.

Two: I was less worried about the risk because of personal taste. I recommend when people first start buying and selling to focus on the items they like, as previously mentioned. If you end up not being able to sell the items, at least you are left with something you will enjoy. It's supposed to be part fun, part money making. I purchased the figures in England and I love *Star Wars*. If I got stuck with them, I'd be left with some cool *Star Wars* action figures in great condition.

But I knew my market and I have several toy contacts who I had in mind before committing. It's key to make sure you know your market. It's like going to a party with a bunch of friends. You don't want to bring a box of alcopops if nobody likes them – bring the drink that you know your friends like.

I can say on record that this was the fastest sale I have ever had in my entire life. I was tracking the delivery on my phone and I could see the truck coming on the GPS. As I was telling a friend that it was coming in, I didn't realise one of the biggest toy dealers around was in the neighbourhood.

He wanted to know all about them, and I was telling him as the figures were being lifted off the truck. As I opened the package, he said, 'I'm buying them. Period. How much do you want?' I already had a price in mind for the 12 and, like that, they went for £3,000 – a £2,200 profit. I had them in my hands for literally 10 seconds before I sold them and tripled my money.

You always want to set yourself up for success. By lowering the risk and knowing your market, when preparation meets opportunity, you have those big moments.

7. Try making antiques modern

There's a new generation of buyers around that don't care much for antiques. But what they can't deny is the craftsmanship of antiques – there's a reason why those pieces of furniture are still around. If you're buying a dresser, for example, it is probably more advantageous for you to check an antiques store, knowing that what you buy is going to last you a long time.

You can do things to these items to make them more contemporary – and you can then choose to keep hold of them for a while and use them, safe in the knowledge that you've potentially added value, which you can cash in at a later date. It doesn't need to look brand new – it's an antique.

People take old wood furniture, whether oak or mahogany, and repaint it to make it look cool – they upcycle it to make it more modern and current. That freshens it up and gives it more value – from a modern standpoint, not from an antique standpoint – while knowing the item is going to last a long time. You have the best of both worlds: a contemporary look *and* longevity.

There is a different generation of buyers looking for quality furniture with a modern look and, with a bit of creativity, you can find these items at antiques centres and upcycle them yourself. In essence, you're shopping for potential, not for antique and collectible purposes, so assess the worth of items from that perspective.

USING THE BLUEPRINT: ANTIQUES CENTRES AND RETRO SHOPS

- Antiques shops and centres will have some untapped gems – hunt for those unloved items that might have been there for a long time.
- Most dealers are out to make profit, just like you, so make sure you haggle properly and attempt to sniff out the value. Items are priced in a way that encourages haggling.
- Plenty of dealers are in this line of work for the fun factor – recognize your dealer and haggle accordingly.
- Try to exploit dealer circumstance to find opportunities for profit.
- Think about your location to work out what might sell well in a local area, and what items a dealer may be struggling to shift.
- Hunt in those nooks and crannies for items that have clearly been sitting there for a long time for extra haggle space.
- Remember that there might be a gem laying under some broken goods, like my glass apothecary bottles.
- Look for those easy wins like precious metals – check the price it is being sold for against its weight and current metal values.
- These places aren't all stuffy antiques and china – keep looking out for your niche items, like my vintage band t-shirts.
- When you're on holiday, pop into retro stores and antiques centres to help pay for your trip.

LESSON 14: ESTATE AND GARAGE SALES – UNTAPPED TREASURE

LEVEL: Intermediate/advanced
PROFIT POTENTIAL: £££

Clubbed together in this lesson are estate sales and garage sales – these are quite different things but, when you think about it, they have a lot in common with either the entire contents of a home or just some of the contents, ready to buy or be taken for absolutely nothing.

Many may have visions of a grand country manor with chandeliers being sold off, or paintings that won't fit into your own modest pile, but that is not the case. Estate sales can be an untapped opportunity to snag items that need to be got rid of quickly, and often cheaply.

Garage sales often see an entire street come together to sell items on pasting tables on their driveways, a kind of lazy boot sale if you will. There has also been an upturn in people simply leaving items outside their home ready for anyone to take away for absolutely nothing.

Estate and garage sales may be different formats, but the mentality of both the buyer and the seller is exactly the same. The seller aims to make money and these types of sales offer an easy avenue to offload your belongings without having to go to specific places like eBay, car boot sales or specialist outlets where they will have to invest more effort and also pay fees. The idea is to clear it all out in the convenience of your own home, all in one go.

From a buyer's perspective, you never know what you're going to find at these sales – but more than likely, you're going to find deals.

WHAT IS IT? THE ESSENTIALS

Estate sales see the contents of a home sold off, often after a death or repossession. If you hold your nerve, they result in some chunky profits.

Quite a few resale pros have a van and offer to clear out homes for free, dumping what they don't want, but keeping anything they like. I have done this quite a bit in my resale life.

Garage sales are more common in the US than Britain – but they are increasingly popular, and can be a treasure trove of items that can be haggled on hard. Unlike a car boot sale, there is no entry fee and homeowners are likely to want to shift stuff pronto.

WHY IT'S WORTH YOUR TIME

I absolutely adore estate sales. That's because it is the first time items have seen the light of day. They haven't even left the home yet and they already have a price tag on them. There's no pre-sorting. There's no setting up to market the item. It's simply people opening the door and letting you walk in and find something that piques your interest. You spot a bargain and there is a bit of back and forth. It is the most organic form of resale.

Garage sales are similar, but just one step further – the items have just left the house.

On the down side, you may have to go through plenty of stuff you're not interested in to try to find a couple of gems, and you will also probably have to travel some distance, making a special trip for just one sale. However, the probability of finding gems is quite significant simply because it's the first raw step. The intended purpose of an estate sale or garage sale is more than likely to get rid of items. These aren't antiques dealers, you're dealing with someone whose main aim is to clear out the house, and nothing more.

PROFIT POTENTIAL

I have made some serious profit at both these types of event – but probably for different reasons. Profits on estate sales are likely to be bigger, as the entire contents of a home are often up for grabs and this can include antique furniture, tech and other pricier items.

When it comes to garage sales, it is more likely to be the typical loot that is on offer at car boot sales, mainly lower-value items. That said, it is easier to move a piece of furniture out onto your driveway to sell than lug it to a car boot sale, so chunky profits shouldn't be ruled out if buyers are lazy.

HOW TO FIND A GOOD ESTATE OR GARAGE SALE

Back in the day, estate sales and garage sales were listed in the classified section of local newspapers. Now you can find them on apps and Facebook Marketplace, so it is worth a scour.

You need to acquire information before you decide whether to go. Google the address and find out where it is, then do some research. Is it in an affluent street? This will probably reflect in the quality of the goods. Is it in the middle of nowhere, where there will be fewer eyes on the goods? Do your research to get an advantage over the competition.

Tips and tricks for success

1. Take advantage of estate sales

Buying at an estate sale is one of my favourite parts of being a resale pro. It's like your own personal game show. The adrenaline factor is huge – what's behind this door? That door? You never know what you're going to find when you walk into people's houses. It is intriguing and exciting, whether or not you make money.

The idea is to go in with a flexible approach. Take advantage of the situation with the knowledge that the seller themself wants you to take advantage: they need the house cleared. You enter, and take away the good stuff.

Sometimes people hire estate companies if they have more high-end stuff to sell. This is more of a speciality resale segment – the profit potential here is scarce, and better suited to more advanced resellers, people who really get into estate sales.

If you know someone has sold their home or someone has died, whether or not an estate sale has been advertised, it can be beneficial for you to ask, 'Are you guys selling anything in the house?' People always have items they don't want when getting rid of a home – whether it is one they've inherited or are selling to downsize, because of a messy divorce or because they've hit financial hard times.

2. Also take advantage of garage sales

People often put signs up to say they're having a garage sale and sometimes a whole street or neighbourhood gets involved. But even if you just see a house up for sale, it never hurts to ask if there is anything they want to sell.

Lee tells me that when he was buying his new home, the previous occupants offered him the white goods, a sofa and a triple wardrobe –

all in great condition – for £1,500. He refused because he didn't think it was a great deal and, given it was his first home, he was happy to buy brand new.

The sellers then offered it all to him for a nominal £50. He gladly accepted. The reality was, their next home also had the white goods already in and it would have been more of a hassle disposing of the stuff than handing it over for next to nothing. Lee could have chosen to simply take all those items out onto the driveway the day he moved in and tried to sell them for a profit (he didn't).

Remember the mantra: everything has value. But for most people, the reality and stress of moving means that you usually have a bunch of stuff you don't want to take with you. What do you do with it? Throw it away, donate it, or give it away. These are opportunities to swoop in.

It doesn't hurt to ask because, worst case scenario, all they can say is no. Best case scenario, however, you could be having some serious score with items that might have been heading to landfill – it puts you in a position to make a profit.

ACTION POINT: Trawl through local forums and social media to find an upcoming estate or garage sale and get it into the diary.

---

3. Connect the dots

The best estate sales are the ones where you can connect the dots using your observations of people's buying habits and styles to predict what you are likely to find. If all their furniture is Ikea, then more than likely, they won't be hiding any antique furniture.

If all their clothes are Primark, you can expect that other things they are buying – say the electronics – are unlikely to be top notch. You create this perception of what kind of stuff this person has in the nooks and crannies that you can't see in that very moment.

It's not always the case, however, and you shouldn't always judge an estate sale by its cover. But 90 per cent of the time, it's true.

4. Get a vibe from the seller

At an estate sale I went to recently, I stepped inside the house and spotted a number of antiques, including some antique furniture, in the living room and kitchen. It was a two-storey home and there were five bedrooms upstairs. These siblings were looking at selling the house as their father had passed away. They were splitting the sale price of this $1 million property.

In the grand scheme of things, they were focusing on their share of the house, not really thinking about making a few extra thousand dollars on the contents. I could tell they wanted to release the burden of getting the home cleared. I could hear it in their tone.

Sometimes, I have a hunch to offer to buy everything   and that's what I did. They were instantly interested so they didn't have to sell everything piecemeal, one item at a time, and have a bunch of random people trawl through the home. Dealing with one person was a savings grace for them but put me in the driver's seat.

5. Look outside the obvious to find a hidden gem

To delve further into the story, what made me make the offer was that I could see a piece of furniture I knew I could get $800 for. I knew when offering $1,500 for the entire contents, my risk was very small. In the end, they settled on $2,000. Without even going upstairs, I said yes and shook on it.

I soon found five other pieces of furniture that I could easily sell for $100 each – so the running total was then $1,300. I was now $700 in the hole, but hadn't even been upstairs yet.

It turns out the dad was an antique radio collector. His office had some radio tubes, which of course I now had knowledge of (see page 109), alongside other miscellaneous equipment. A box of silver coins in his office drawer was worth $1,000 alone.

But, the big find – the hidden gem – was an old RCA microphone in pieces (the one I mentioned earlier). I knew nothing about it at the time. I took the pieces to a man in Pasadena, California, the most world-renowned vintage microphone repair guy. I paid $400 for him to repair it and sold it for $1,900.

Other items like the radio tubes and some other miscellaneous super-niche equipment went to an auction house. All in all, I made $10,000 from that $2,000 investment.

DISNEY HAUL WAS NO CHILD'S PLAY

One Friday, a friend of mine asked if I wanted to go with him to a garage sale the next morning. It was posted online on a local app, which showed a tiny thumbnail of the contents. I could make out a giant Budweiser neon sign, along with some other porcelain signs and a big cast-iron item, on which I recognized a pattern in the metal.

This app had his email address, so I sent a message: 'Would you be interested in selling me these items before your sale happens?'. He replied immediately and said, if I came in the next hour, he'd consider it. So on the Friday evening, I went to the address. I ended up being there until the early hours of the morning after discovering a treasure trove of goods.

After he loosened up a bit, he told me about some boxes of Disney goods and vintage Coca-Cola items he had. It transpired that his mum was one of the very first Coca-Cola salespeople for the fast food industry and her favourite pastime was going to Disneyland and keeping every imaginable item that had Mickey's face on it, from sugar packets to perfume bottles. She kept every single item that she bought there.

I bought his entire garage sale. I initially thought I was going to spend $50–$80 but I parted with $10,000 and, in the end, he never had the garage sale. But the return I've made on that outing has been insane. As a conservative estimate, I've made a five-fold profit on it, and all because I messaged the guy over a thumbnail image of items I saw and the fact that I recognized that what was in those two boxes was unique – especially the Disney items.

Much of it has ended up being drip-fed to auctions. The most recent one garnered me $2,000 on a few items. Some of the items were unique pieces from the 1950s and 1960s but there was also 1920s stuff in there. When you look at the Disney copyright stamp, it usually just reads 'Disney'. When it starts getting older, it says 'Walt Disney'. This 1920s stuff reads 'Walter E Disney', making it super-rare and hard to find.

At one point, I received a call from the Disney head office and they sent people to come and check out some of the goods I had. They bought some of it – I guess bits they didn't have. I had signed internal documents from Disneyland, blueprints, maps – including the original Disneyland map in fantastic condition. I sold that for $500.

There were figurines and loads of toys from the 1960s and 1970s still in their boxes, untouched, as well as animation folders signed by animators. It was a once-in-a-lifetime opportunity and I just took advantage.

It all started with me wanting to buy a Budweiser neon sign. I have to emphasize it: I have nothing special, all I'm doing is trying to follow a path finding items that are forgotten or people just want to get rid of. I take advantage of the opportunities as they come. I'm not bragging, I'm just using a real-world example to show how anyone can do this.

6. Consider potential loss leaders

In previous lessons, I have been stressing the importance of the quick wins, buying items you know you can sell on quickly. For beginners, it's vital, but still holds true the more experienced you get. Most of what I buy and sell are things I think I can offload quickly.

However, sometimes at estate and garage sales, people just want to get rid of stuff fast. You can offer to ease their burden by buying everything, but at reduced price, even if you know that some of it might not be worth much and you have no plan for where you can sell it on.

I'm not saying be a bag holder, but sometimes it pays to treat some items as a bit of a loss leader. The idea is that you are lessening the cost of the things you actually want. It's a win-win. Some of the items in a bulk buy won't be worth your time or effort, but you're masking the items that are valuable and getting them for a lower price by buying it all.

If you say you're going to take everything, often you'll get a better deal than if you just focus on the good stuff – the rubbish items are masking the true value of it all. In turn, this should give you more overall value.

Don't take on more than you can chew, however, but you want to look like you're not going to just pillage people, going into their house, gutting them and taking the good stuff. It's almost like you're doing them a favour by taking it all, when in fact you've seen a few items that are going to get your outlay back. The rest is bonus profit.

7. Be first or last

Like car boot sales, I recommend being first or last to an estate or garage sale. If you're first, you'll have free pick. If you're last, you have a great opportunity to snag some stuff for free.

Again, it is just a matter of asking the right questions. Ask what they are going to do with all this stuff when the sale is finished. I've lost count of the number of times people have just told me to take it away, because they don't want to lug it back inside, or simply asked for a nominal fee for it.

It's unlikely these will be quality items worth hundreds of pounds. But they could be decent items that you could sell at a car boot sale, online, or through barcode-scanning apps to turn a nice little profit.

I'll give you a recent example. At one estate sale, I spotted around a dozen cardboard boxes full of CDs. It was the end of the day and the owners were just going to toss them – no one listens to CDs anymore, right? It's all about streaming.

I gave them a couple of bucks for around 800 CDs, loaded them into my car, went home and scanned the barcodes as I ate a sandwich and watched television. I made around $100 for about half of them and sent them off in a pre-paid envelope. A little bit of work for a $95 return. It's so simple.

USING THE BLUEPRINT: ESTATE AND GARAGE SALES

As you can see, it is well worth visiting people in their homes to try to do deals on the items they no longer want. I've made some huge profits this way. Don't be afraid to ask questions and to hunt down those items that are going to turn you profits, big and small.

- Go into these events with flexibility to do a deal and take advantage of the situation.
- Someone moving? Get in touch and see if there is anything they're selling to get ahead of the curve.
- Look outside the obvious – yes, the antique furniture is worth plenty, but there could be untapped gems.
- Minimize risk by totting up the value of items and potentially offering a sum of money to take the lot.
- Again, it can pay to be first or last to these events.

LESSON 15: SPECIALITY AUCTIONS – FROM LOST LUGGAGE TO CURRENCY CRAZINESS

LEVEL: Advanced
PROFIT POTENTIAL: £££

Many of you will recognize me from *Storage Hunters* – either the US or the UK version of the show in which I – along with a range of other characters – bid on storage containers, not knowing for sure what lurks inside.

The question I get asked all the time is: was it real? While of course some of it was created to make good television, it was real – my own cash was on the line and I was there to bid on containers for potential profits. I used to bid on containers before the show began, and still do it from time to time to this day.

People can bankrupt themselves buying these units but, like a game of poker, there are always winners. It taught me a number of tricks and tips that I will now pass on to you.

There are plenty of speciality auctions around and – let me tell you something – quite often, they have a low turnout because they are often during working hours, making them awkward for the nine-to-five crowd without some serious forward planning.

I love the random nature of these auctions, with items big and small being sold at them. Many are physical auctions, but some of them are also online – or can be accessed online while the physical auction is taking place.

In Britain, many associate speciality auctions with television programmes like *Homes Under the Hammer*. Although I'm sure money can be made buying derelict, run-down property, it comes with considerable risks and a skill set above my remit. Everything else is on the table though.

WHAT IS IT? THE ESSENTIALS

Storage auctions aren't all that common in Britain, compared with the US. Essentially, these are lock-ups where people store goods but, for whatever reason, they've abandoned them and stopped paying the rent. The last resort for the company is to auction off the contents to make up for lost rental income. These auctions are usually held online or at auction houses, and you are likely to have some indication as to what is lurking inside.

But that aside, there are a number of fascinating auctions you can go to and find interesting items, applying some of the skills I learned on *Storage Hunters*. There are auctions selling off lost luggage items from airports, stolen items retrieved by the police, and specialist auctions for goods such as currency, as well as collectibles such as artwork, clocks, historical artefacts, militaria, and movie and sports memorabilia.

WHY IT'S WORTH YOUR TIME

Speciality auctions can be a great spot to find hidden bargains, but I would argue that out of all the Part III lessons, this is the one most geared towards an advanced level of resale. That is, you'll likely be coming up against seasoned professionals who know exactly what they're looking for, in a sometimes rushed atmosphere. There is more of a risk of making a costly mistake here, with many people having their auction experience shaped by what they've seen on television.

But, if you can find a good auction – one that might be relatively empty of buyers given the time of day or year – take some of my advice and ignore the razzmatazz, they can be great places to build contacts and find some hidden gems.

Some of these auctions are held online, or you can make online bids, so you might not need to attend in person, making them an efficient use of your time. Recent data suggests auctions are booming as more people become comfortable browsing items online rather than seeing them in person.

PROFIT POTENTIAL

Depending on the circumstances, the profit potential can be huge, but I'll point this out once more: this type of event is largely for those with experience.

Once you've learned the ropes at boot sales, charity shops and antiques stores, you're more likely to succeed at an event like this and make money. There are a number of ways to take advantage.

HOW TO FIND GOOD SPECIALITY AUCTIONS

The internet is key here – both in finding events and in checking out reviews, to see what the general vibe is.

There are many great aggregate websites out there now listing speciality auctions. Auction houses across the country sign up for these sites and they usually have a search option so you can look up certain items and genres. For example, I recently typed in '*Star Wars* toys' and was then taken to an auction house in Central England.

Sometimes, niche items appear in non-speciality auctions. I recently found some Nintendo gaming watches worth £200 each. Instead of being at a Nintendo auction, or even a video game auction, they were in a general auction. I bought some of them for £5 each. It's well worth using those search tools. These websites have brought auction houses into the 21st century.

ACTION POINT: Have a look at some of those aggregate websites listed in the Resources section at the end of this lesson and hunt down a niche genre or item.

Tips and tricks for success

1. Learn to spot the good signs

So how do you decide whether to bid at lost luggage auctions, police auctions, coin auctions and other niche auctions when you don't know what you are buying? For example, at a lost luggage auction, can you be sure a Louis Vuitton bag will have some designer goods inside?

Whenever I am bidding blind on a storage container or other auction, my focus is always to lower my risk and use the information I do have to inform my decision. I also use my knowledge and experience of items that I've dealt with in the past to lower my risk.

For example, I have £1,000 in my pocket to potentially bid on a unit. If I can spot a PlayStation in that unit, I know I can get £150 for it. Now my risk is £850 for the things I can't see. Next I spot a television, for which I can get £100, so my risk is down to £750. Next I see a couple of antiques – general run-of-the-mill stuff – and experience tells me I'm now only risking about £400 on the items I can't see.

Let's say there's about 20 boxes in there and I can't see what's inside. If I divide the amount of risk left – about £400 – by the number of boxes, each box would have to contain £20 of profit for me to break even. This seems incredibly reasonable to me so I would go ahead and bid that £1,000.

I would feel even more confident because I've identified a PlayStation and television and it's a reasonable assumption that the person who was able to afford those, not to mention abandon them, is unlikely to have junk in all those boxes. It still could be all junk, of course, but the likelihood is there will be a build-up of antiques, household wares and saleable kitchen appliances.

RISK FACTOR
LIST OF IDENTIFIABLE ITEMS & VALUE

1. _____ £ _____
2. _____ £ _____
3. _____ £ _____
4. _____ £ _____

THE GUARANTEE £ _____

TOTAL COST – GUARANTEE = £ RISK FACTOR TOTAL

2. Find your unfair advantage

Whether it's an online auction or a physical one, look for easy ways to obtain unfair advantages. Before you start bidding, think how can you find your unfair advantage. Now with online auctions, this will be calling the actual auction house and speaking to them about some of the items you're interested in.

The more information you have, the easier it is for you to make a decision. In many instances, photographs don't tell the full story. The item could be much better – or worse – than the pictures show. Getting that information allows you to make more informed decisions.

3. Use a poker face when bidding

I once bought a £5 note for more than £1,000. It was one of the riskiest buys of my life. The new polymer £5 note had launched in Britain with Winston Churchill on it. Each has an eight-digit serial code on it and the first run of notes, with AA01 prefixes, were selling for big bucks online.

This led me to the Bank of England charity auction, with low-serial-number notes on offer (number AA01 0001 goes to the Queen by the way). The lowest note on offer at this auction was AA01 000017, the lowest one available to the public. It had a reserve of £800–£1,200, but it sold for too much – £4,150, or some 82,900 per cent mark-up on its face value. I didn't want to get dragged into a bidding war as the price escalated.

There are two ways to go about bidding in an auction setting like this – you're a leader or a follower. If you have the money to back up what you're doing, then you can set the pace of the bidding. If the pace of an auction is slow, I will usually speed it up just to throw people off. And vice versa – if people are going fast, I'll slow it down just to throw them off as well. I'm not agitating people for the sake of agitation, but for the sake of value and trying to get those deals. You want to make other bidders feel a little uncomfortable, especially if there are a number of items you plan to bid on. They are your enemy.

With Bank of England notes, there's little outside data you can use to work out the potential value of the things you are bidding on, at least with £5 notes. This new note launched, AA01 note prices went crazy on online marketplaces and then, whoosh, I'm at an auction bidding on a note for far more than face value.

In a circumstance like this I never lead the bidding because you're establishing the price for lot number one. It's effectively a brand new product and the price it achieves will set the standard of prices for the following lots.

When the bidding starts on subsequent lots, in the middle upper tier, there will still be lots of buyers but you try to recognize those who have already had their fill and bought the item they want. Then it's safe to be a second leader, if you will. Think of it in terms of warfare – once the generals and high-ranking guys go out, the low level sergeants are next in line.

It's better to blend in with everyone else rather than being the first one as you risk being the bag holder. If the top tier item isn't as hot as you anticipated, you could be left with a huge loss. If you're in the middle upper tier and an item does really well, you are close enough to the forefront to make a good profit, but you don't have too much invested and risk a big loss.

I was in lightning-in-a-bottle territory with the Bank of England note auction. That's what you're trying to do, catch lightning in a bottle to find a big win. But if you set yourself up with 100 bottles, sooner or later one of those bottles is going to catch that lightning. You're increasing the chances.

Instead of me buying the top tier, number one bank note and taking a big risk on a single item, I bought five of them from three different tiers. Now all of a sudden, I can use the lower-tier item to cover my costs for the upper-tier item and reduce my risk. And I had a great pay out.

That £5 note was a 'fad' buy I wouldn't usually get involved with as the value can easily drop, but pristine notes are always popular with collectors and tend to soar in price.

At the time I believed that putting them in a safe for the future would be the most sensible option. I'd seen a 1955 £5 note with serial number Y71 000001 sell for an incredible £35,000 a few years before. However, as I prefer to keep fluid and nimble and take that quick meaty profit, I ended up selling the five notes for a total of £7,200. My AA01 000020 note went for roughly £4,000, and the other four notes for around £1,000 each. Not bad for a total outlay of roughly £2,000.

That fad has died a death now, with similar £10 note and £20 note auctions not capturing the imagination in quite the same way. Recent eBay sales of AA01 notes have tailed off too. Maybe in 50 years' time, the notes would have been worth a five-figure sum, but I'm too impatient for that kind of wait!

4. Build those bridges

You have to strike a balance between faking it and acting confident while you are starting out and being humble and knowing your limitations. That's why I was the most successful bidder on *Storage Hunters*, simply because I was able to balance playing the persona with a more humble side, still being prepared to use my resources and find opportunities to take things even further.

One of the main things I did was to maintain contact with anyone I interacted with as far as a transaction was concerned, rather than burning bridges and thinking it was a one-off deal. I've nurtured those contacts to this day and can still make use of them when I need them.

Not so long ago, I came across a unit with bumper cars inside. Instantly, I had a buyer in mind before I even started bidding – a guy in Hollywood who sells quirky, unusual items. Rather brilliantly, his name is Miles. That first transaction with him went well. I bought the unit, sold the bumper cars to Miles as I'd hoped, made a profit.

But the money was irrelevant in the grand scheme of things because I was able to do deals with him further down the line – I ended up buying and selling vintage and unusual signs to him to the point where he was retiring and he asked me if I wanted to buy his entire business. This is a prime example of establishing and nurturing those contacts.

There's another guy who bought a slot machine from me. I established a rapport with him and then sold him slot machines two or three more times. Knowing that he repairs them, I started picking up derelict slot machines, usually for around $10. I would send them to him to fix for $50–$100 and then sell them on for upwards of $500. Sometimes, those contacts can be more important than just making money on the first transaction.

5. Learn from your mistakes

You know at job interviews, they often ask, 'What's your biggest flaw?'
You sit there, scratching your head, trying to avoid giving an answer
that might deny you the job. Well, I am happy and open to admit that
my biggest flaw is my ambition. Really, it is. Let me explain why.

Sometimes, ambition gets me in a heap of trouble. This trouble
usually takes one of two forms. The first is getting excited about
electronics that I believe are 'still in the box'. The box fools me into
thinking that they are in mint condition and have just been thrown
into a storage unit or house unused. I made this mistake a few times
while bidding on storage containers.

But I constantly have to remember that that's not how it works in
real life. It's blatantly obvious that the first thing you do when you buy
a television is to take it out of the box. Not everyone is Jesse and keeps
their items like that.

The second is vehicles. If I see an old rusty vehicle, it looks like a
classic car to me. I think, *Man, this car is super-cool*. But reality check
– it's only super-cool when it is completely restored and back on the
road. I really know nothing about repairing cars.

I once sent Mike Brewer – from television show *Wheeler Dealers* –
photographs of a Volkswagen campervan I found for sale (a different
one from the one mentioned earlier – I still hadn't learned). I knew it
would look perfect once done. The conversation went a little like this:

Mike: Dude, there's no floor.

Jesse: Yes, but you could fix it up for me and we can sell it for a profit.

Mike: It will cost too much to fix. Don't do it.

It was lucky I had someone with such expertise to tell me I'd be
crazy. A large purchase like a vehicle can be a profit- and time-zapper.
You've got to know your limitations, remember the value of your time
and not get caught in the romance of an item.

6. Learn to tackle blind-bid auctions

Let's take Heathrow's lost-luggage auctions as an example here. Imagine there are 200 suitcases at the auction one day. This scenario is like bidding blind on a storage unit – you are dealing with a complete question mark. That is, the gamble far outweighs any information you have to go on when making a decision on whether to bid and how much.

It's best to forget about the item itself – there's nothing you can learn from it – and just focus on the people you are bidding against. It's very much like poker – how can you win a poker hand without even looking at your cards? How can I find an opportunity or advantage over the other bidders there? There are going to be people on their game and you want to swoop in and get a deal, irrelevant of what the item is.

Study the other people you're bidding against and ask yourself how they feel about their cards. Do they look confident? Anxious? You might get some clues as to how the bidding will go. If everyone else has junk cards, it doesn't matter what you have, because if you swoop in you could win the bidding for a nominal price.

I've done that many times in the storage auction game, but I've also done it at general auctions too. Whether it's a mystery box or a random piece of furniture or a storage unit, I'm just focused on the other people. It doesn't matter what's inside because I know my spend is going to be minimal.

The mystery box bid piques the interest of the human psyche. It can be fun but don't forget the potential to make huge money isn't always there. Let's not downplay the thrill of these gamble-type auctions – there's always the potential for a massive score – but don't deviate from your game plan of mitigating risk while focusing on maximizing profits.

ACTION POINT: Pop your online auction cherry – find a general or speciality auction and watch the action unfold. It's up to you if you want to buy first time around, or just observe.

SIFTING THROUGH THE JUNK

When I buy a storage unit, I know there's no way it's all going to be gems and top-quality stuff. I've had plenty of auctions where I've made no money at all. I've even had a few auctions where I've lost money. However, I've gained small profits from the majority, albeit alongside a huge amount of work. If you buy a unit and it is full of trash, it is up to you to clear it out and dispose of it, otherwise you are charged a huge cleaning fee.

Everything does have value, but I've come across literal trash, like food items and soiled goods. People store the weirdest stuff. I've come across bodily fluids, bones and ashes before – although, at least I managed to sell the urn on.

I can't stress enough that this isn't a get-rich-quick book. There can be plenty of work involved. But the great news is, you don't need anything to make these potential profits other than your own hard work. You don't need a degree to unearth money-making opportunities, just plenty of elbow grease.

7. Don't write anything off

Some buyers and sellers devalue items straight away, simply because they don't have the knowledge or experience to deal with them. For example, video games aren't for everyone and wouldn't appeal to, say, an antiques expert buying fancy Parisian lamps. Essentially, the value to that person is zero.

I felt a bit like that when I came across some old cameras in a storage unit. But just because I didn't know anything about them, I didn't just write them off. I turned them into a new branch of my knowledge tree.

You never really get to know the full story behind a storage unit. They are usually at auction because the previous owners didn't make the payments – they fell behind and the unit was repossessed. It's usually people who have fallen on hard times, been sent to jail, died, got divorced, moved overseas or gone into the military. I've seen it all.

I made $42,000 on that one unit and the cameras were a key component. In one box I found five vintage Leica cameras that I sold to the president of a camera club in Massachusetts. It made me appreciate the idea that there really is something for everyone. I had little idea how collectible vintage cameras were. However, it reminded me once again not to write things off. Some people out there have a serious passion for certain items.

BIDDING TIPS FOR ONLINE AUCTIONS

If you're bidding online – whether it's an online-only auction or part of a live auction that you cannot attend in person – just because you cannot see faces, doesn't mean you don't need a poker face.

I treat online bidding the same way as if I'm attending an actual auction. When there's lots of quick bidding, I try to slow it down as much as possible. When there's long drawn out bidding, I try to bid as quickly as possible, unsettling the other bidders.

These speciality auctions can get oversaturated. If you have an auction that, say, just deals with *Star Wars* toys, many of the mid-tier and lower-mid-tier items are overlooked because bidders are only focused on the top-tier items.

Most of the time, I don't even bother with the first few lots as everyone's so focused on them. Instead, I try to find value somewhere in the middle, when bidders are feeling overwhelmed or they've already spent all their money on the big-time stuff. Let's say there are 500 lots in the same category. There is going to be fatigue when you get to lot 300, or lot 400. That's a ripe time to swoop in and find opportunity.

I'll give you a real-life example. I used to bid online for arcade machines and one auction I bid on had 700 machines. It started at noon. Each lot takes between three and four minutes. What I would often do in these auctions is get involved later in the day, knowing that the number of people bidding from noon to 2pm, or 2pm to 5pm, will be significantly higher than those bidding from midnight to 2am.

I mean, only crazy people hunting profits are up in the small hours bidding on arcade machines. The quality of goods is nowhere near that at the beginning of the day, but who cares about the quality of goods when the potential profit margin is massive?

Essentially, you're buying a machine for £50 and selling it for £200, instead of buying it for £1,800 and selling it for £2,000. It's better from a risk perspective and a potential profit perspective. Taking advantage of buyer fatigue is a great way to swoop in for profits. And don't forget to glean as much information as you can about the items before bidding starts to give you an advantage over some of the other bidders.

USING THE BLUEPRINT: SPECIALITY AUCTIONS

It's all about finding those unfair advantages in these situations, whether you are bidding in person or online. Remember to hold your nerve and take advantage of bidder fatigue. This can be quite an advanced level of resale, as you may be up against seasoned professionals.

- Use apps to hunt down auctions and specific items and genres for sale at auctions.
- Look out for niche items at non-speciality auctions.
- Lowering your risk is key – balance how much you spend with how much you think items are worth.
- There are two types of bidder at auctions, the leader and the follower. Establish which one you're going to be.
- It can pay to sit out the top-tier lots at the beginning of an auction and focus on mid-tier items to let the serious bidders exit.
- Build contacts at these events, don't burn bridges – often these contacts are far more important in the long term than that first interaction you have with them.
- Don't get caught in the romance of an item, especially something chunky and hard to move on, like a vehicle (unless you have the skills and expertise). Stick in your lane.
- You might need to put in plenty of hard work at these events to turn profits. It's not all quick wins and easy money.
- Don't write items off. You can usually find someone somewhere who'll want to buy it.
- Bidding online? Make sure you still have a poker face to play the room correctly.
- What is your unfair advantage going to be? Make use of all the resources and information you can get your hands before bidding starts.
- Take advantage of buyer fatigue. At a long, drawn-out auction, it can pay to come in later in the day.

RESOURCES

Invaluable (www.invaluable.com) – a website listing upcoming auctions worldwide with online bidding

The Sale Room (www.the-saleroom.com) – a website listing upcoming auctions worldwide with online bidding

Easy Live Auction (www.easyliveauction.com) – a website listing upcoming auctions worldwide with online bidding

Spink (www.spink.com) – auctions of currency and other collectibles with online bidding

Bumblebee (www.bumblebeeauctions.co.uk) – UK police property disposal auctions

Greasbys (www.greasbys.co.uk) – London auction house with lost luggage auctions

BCVA commercial auctions (www.thebcva.co.uk) – UK auction house with lost luggage auctions

LESSON 16: THE INTERNET – THE GOOD, THE BAD AND THE UGLY

LEVEL: Intermediate
PROFIT POTENTIAL: £££

The good old world wide web. When it comes to resale, many people go straight to the internet – with a few taps of a keyboard and clicks of a mouse, you can present your item to an international audience. But the internet can be both really good and really bad for resale, which I will explain in more detail in this lesson.

There is a danger of wasting too much time messing about making items look and sound perfect. You are essentially parked on the sofa not out there in the resale game, which is more what I'm about. But if you're struggling to shift something locally or via your contacts, it can be a huge benefit to have that wider buyer base.

The internet really is the Wild West. We'll reveal the good, the bad and the ugly.

WHAT IS IT? THE ESSENTIALS

I often think about that David Bowie clip in which he is interviewed by Jeremy Paxman in the early 2000s. He talks about the potential power of the internet, before it was really grasped by the general population, stating the 'unimaginable' implications it would have on society. That was when I was really starting my resale life and Bowie captures perfectly just how quickly the technological age has burst upon us.

Unless you've lived under a rock for the last two decades, you'll know what the internet is. From a resale perspective, I treat it as a door into another room for you to find and connect with people. It offers endless opportunity and resources.

But how do you make your time and effort on the internet more efficient? It largely boils down to Googling better. Before you jump on the motorway, you make sure you have a map and identify your direction. Before you start on the internet, you need to establish how you are going to identify the buyer who will pay the most for your item, without taking a wrong turn and ending up wasting time.

The search engine is your friend and your starting point. If you are trying to sell your phone, where are you located? Instead of Googling 'sell phone', search for 'sell phone in Lancashire'. Now you have a direction, or at least a general direction.

When you start looking at the search results, other factors come into play – namely, how much is this person likely to pay? Then you have to think about your time. Do you have to send it off to someone? Do they have to approve it? Do they have to send you payment and then wait for it to come? Is there somewhere local to you, within ten minutes, where they'll give you instant cash?

Now you're starting to establish your step one, step two, step three, step four, step five to get to your destination. The internet is usually step one on your road to reach a sale.

WHY IT'S WORTH YOUR TIME

The internet is a great tool and resource for instant valuing, instant selling, instant buying and instant information. However, it is only a great tool if you use your time correctly, don't fall into the resale rabbit holes or end up losing focus. You also come across timewasters and scammers.

As time goes by, I find myself using the internet less and less in terms of actually buying and selling. Face-to-face transactions are more important for me, simply because of their speed and simplicity, as I'll explain.

That said, don't just write the internet off completely – milk it for all the information you can get.

PROFIT POTENTIAL

How long is a piece of string? The profit potential is there, but remember online selling usually involves fees, hidden costs, postage and packaging, and plenty more profit killers.

However, on the odd occasion, it can result in fresh eyes on an item from far and wide, especially when it gets to the end of the road for an item you really want to get rid of.

HOW TO FIND GOOD WEBSITES

I have a resale folder on my smartphone filled with apps I use frequently. These apps have made competition fierce and you want these companies to compete for your business.

Ask yourself which app is going to outdo the other one to get your business. Spend a bit of time finding the best platforms for buying or selling. Most people's first thought will be eBay and this marketplace has grown hugely since the birth of dotcom usage. However, it faces threats from other websites such as Facebook Marketplace.

There are also other useful tools online, such as valuation websites, forums to help you spot trends and bargains, quick apps for quick cash and ones to help find specialist auctions almost instantly.

Tips and tricks for success

Disclaimer: I'm not a huge online seller (anymore).

I do buy and sell online, don't get me wrong. But it's not really my thing anymore – it's a small part of my resale life compared to physical and face-to-face transactions. But I did use it more in my earlier years. I even used to sell free coupons I found on the internet…on the internet. I just made them more easily accessible.

To be in the resale game, you need to find your passion and use the resources available to you to be successful. These are the two key things, whether you are selling online or in the real world. I've seen so many people take the cart-before-the-horse approach – money first then passion, drive and desire second.

I've met hardcore swap meet people who weren't swap meet people at all. They were internet people who were buying items on the internet to sell on at these events. They had this fallacy of value that meant they were just being glorified bag holders.

As I mentioned earlier, I met a guy selling fidget spinners at $3 apiece. He told me he had 10,000 of them, bought for 50 cents each. He was five grand in the hole, still trying to recover his costs and he had no idea what to do. The guy was trying to make money selling fidgets spinners, when in reality he was trying to get out of selling fidgets spinners.

I've said it a million times and I'll say it a million more – you need to mitigate risk, especially with the internet, because there are so many scams and tricks out there. You want to find an area to carve out knowledge – or if not knowledge, at least have the connections to supply that knowledge for you. Then you should never be left as the bag holder.

Keep those basic principles in mind before you even start Googling, before you even log into the computer. You need to understand the basic concepts of knowing what you're getting yourself into, having some basic understanding of price points, and the potential ways to sell your goods. Then you set yourself up and your probability of success grows.

1. CHOOSE YOUR STYLE OR BE A HYBRID

When it comes to resale in the modern age, most people have a hybrid style. It's unwise to discount any method of buying and selling. I just met a guy who's been buying and selling vintage clothes for 30 years. And the most technology he uses? Business cards.

That's how uncomplicated his resale game is and he's one of the most successful vintage clothes dealers in Southern California. He's not being naïve, he just stays in his lane and understands his opportunities, knowing what he's capable of and pushing forward with that. You have to decide what you're willing and not willing to do, recognize your personal limitations and education and take things one step at a time.

Whether you want to sell at an antique stores or car boot sale, on Instagram or eBay, you need to identify the outlet that gives you the biggest probability of success in terms of turning a profit. You'll want to establish which platform allows you to do that as efficiently and quickly as possible to maximize profits. The internet might not be my bread and butter. But it might be yours.

2. FIND YOUR MARKET

The internet has changed the resale game in the last 20 years. I can now buy from and sell to anyone in the world, whether they are next door or on the other side of the planet. This is great from a buying perspective as you have more choices and you're able to lower your costs.

But from a seller's perspective it may come across as a bit scary, knowing that you have a massive increase in competition. However, on the flip side, you also have a massive increase in customers – you can reach more people.

As long as you find your market, you should be successful – whether it's an untapped market or just an opportunity for a quick in and out. If you buy something as a one-time flip based on opportunity and value, if you have awareness of your market, success should come your way.

Things won't always work out, of course. I estimate that 1–3 per cent of the stuff I buy doesn't sell, and I end up donating it or swapping it for something else. When you start out, this is likely to be far higher. As we've already seen, you just need to keep your risk low to minimize inventory decay.

3. KNOW YOUR AUDIENCE

There are three types of seller. First are the old timers with rotary telephones who don't use computers whatsoever. You then have generation one – these are people who use quintessential resources like eBay, Google and the big-name players they've grown up with.

Then there is generation two, people who look past these obvious places and use platforms catering to more specific needs and requirements, especially apps and those with low fees. Most people fail to understand that there is usually a niche market for something that you're particularly interested in.

Right now, I'm not selling on eBay at all. All my stuff goes to private auction houses around the world. As I write this, I have sports cards going to an auction next month in Quebec. I have porcelain signs and other items going into an auction in Chicago, and antique radio equipment that I'm delivering to Burbank, California. I am shipping some American military memorabilia to a speciality auction house in Northampton and have recently snapped up some vinyl records at an auction in Rayleigh. As rapper Ludacris (almost) sang, 'I've got goods, I've got goods, in different area codes.'

You would never hear of these companies without a little searching and being creative, yet you have a better chance of turning a higher profit or selling quicker on these niche platforms than on eBay.

The internet is a huge resource and eBay is not the be-all-and-end-all of internet sales. Generation one, especially, needs to get out of that mindset. Know your audience. Don't sell baby boomer antiques on Gen Z apps, or vice versa.

4. LEARN AND EVOLVE, LIKE KATY PERRY

As mentioned before, I'm not a huge one for selling on the internet, but I do use it to learn. If you have a specific product, we recommend going to YouTube to find out whether or not someone has tried it before. If you're thinking about going down a particular resale route, it's more than likely that someone has already thought of it and documented what they have done on YouTube.

Now, if you have something that is brand new, awesome. Well done. It could potentially work out and be record breaking, who knows. But if you can identify someone who is doing something similar to you, you can extract information.

It's not always about being creative and doing something brand new and fresh. It can be just as profitable to replicate someone else's success because they've already done the work for you. You can then evolve the idea into your own.

Most pop music sounds the same – someone takes one of the core eight pop background tracks and turns it into their own hit. Be a Katy Perry or Justin Bieber. Sample those beats, using the resources available right now, and turn them into your own mega hit.

Don't gauge your success on originality or how many likes you get from others. Focus on the goal, the wins – no matter how big – and stay the course.

5. CHECK PRICES ONLINE

It's always good to double-check values to see what something really is worth. I always undervalue my items, simply to avoid disappointment later. It's about having that self-awareness. There's plenty of misinformation out there, though, so stay alert and recognize that certain websites may not carry realistic information, and that asking prices are not the same as sold prices, to manage your expectations.

I am always gathering as much data as I can from as many different sources as possible to build up a realistic picture. For example, you might be searching for recent sales data for item A, and find that one of them sold for £100, ten of them sold for £50, and one of them sold for £30. With a little maths, you can now base your valuation on 12 different sales, making an educated guess of what item A might be worth.

There are two main resources I constantly use. The first is eBay sold data, which shows the last 30 to 60 days of sales of a specific item. But I also have an invaluable subscription to a website called Worth Point, which has historical data from the last 10–15 years of all eBay sales, as well as specific auction houses. It costs money, but once you get into an advanced level of resale, it is worth the outlay.

But what's to stop someone from creating a dummy eBay account and buying their own items at an inflated price to skew the sold data? Nothing – we see it all the time with items like coins. The item could be listed as sold for £1,000, when in reality it's only worth £100. When a genuine buyer checks the sold prices, they would find that one similar to the item they are interested in recently sold for £1,000, when in reality the price was artificially hiked up.

Of course eBay stamps down on this kind of behaviour, but unfortunately scam artists are constantly evolving on all manner of resale websites. It's one of the potential pitfalls of the internet but it can still be an important tool for understanding value.

6. LOOK LOCALLY TOO

Try Googling an item and typing in the word 'sold' after it, or type in the item name and 'for sale'. For example, try 'PlayStation 4 sold' or 'PlayStation 4 for sale'. You will often discover websites you have never heard of where people are selling that item.

You might find more local sites, classified ads, some apps you've never heard of – and all the information you can amass will help you get a clearer understanding of what an item is selling for at that specific point in time.

7. CHOOSE THE RIGHT KEYWORDS AND CATEGORIES

If you do end up listing an item on an online marketplace, there are a number of easy tips and tricks to maximize the number of eyes on your product, and its profit potential.

Make sure you use the right keywords, list it in the correct category and be detailed about its condition or anything that makes it unique or stand out. Great photographs are important, too, as we've pointed out previously.

You may also want to consider listing your item on a Sunday evening. According to data from eBay, the busiest time for buyers is Sunday evenings. And December is the busiest month.

ACTION POINT: List an item online on a Sunday evening. But first master the art of keywords, categories, descriptions and photographs. Take inspiration from others selling similar items – see what they do right, and what looks bad.

INTERNET PITFALLS

The internet can be one giant pitfall – it's just a matter of how far you fall. Take it one step at a time to avoid major disasters.

Don't buy in bulk for the sake of buying in bulk, and try to buy from a reputable source. If you're thinking of buying from a particular website, go to Google, type in the name of the website and add the word 'review' to see what others are saying.

You can also get reviews on specific platforms. Type in the platform name, then type in the word 'forum' and you should find message boards where people can post messages specifically on that platform. Do your research on the platform, as well as on specific items, to prevent you from any issues down the line with the payment process, dealing with scams or shipping procedures.

Let me give you a cautionary tale. A man contacted me in a frenzy of excitement. He had a silver $1 coin. These things can sell for big bucks. When he brought it to show me, I took one look and had to stifle a giggle. The face on the coin was all off – it had a huge chin. He'd bought it off the internet for far too much money, and it was clearly a knock-off.

Remember that quite often on the internet, if something looks too good to be true, it probably is.

WHEN I DID USE EBAY TO SCORE A $6,500 PROFIT

I had a connection with an employee at Santa Barbara zoo. One day, I was visiting for fun and bumped into them. As we were chatting about this and that, they happened to mention they were getting a brand new lion enclosure and the kids' play area was being cleared out to make room. Unsurprisingly, lions and children don't mix awfully well.

They asked if I knew anyone who does removal of metal and other playground equipment. It turned out they had a kids' carousel, eight feet wide and ten feet tall, with four animals on it. What were they going to do with that? Well, they had no idea. I went and had a look and, after showing some interest, was simply asked, 'What's your best price?'

It was a lovely carousel, in great condition and unique. I offered $500, a real lowball offer, fully expecting a no. The manager was consulted and I was told I had a deal. But...only if I could take it away that day. I agreed without understanding the logistics of a one-and-a-half tonne carousel. I had to dismantle it, break it down, get the motor out, load it into my vehicle, drive down to my house and then set it back up again.

This was a rare occasion in my recent resale career when I didn't actually have a buyer in mind. Instead, I simply went for it because it was super-cool and a real bargain. I loaded up before they could change their mind. I then listed it on eBay for $20,000. Yes, you read that right, $20,000. Because of the effort involved and the uniqueness, I simply tested the water.

I then lowered it to $18,000, $15,000, $12,000 then $11,000. After six months, not one person messaged me and this clunky thing was taking up too much room in my backyard. It's a classic example of why I prefer to have a buyer lined up before I commit.

When it was priced at $9,000, a guy finally contacted me. He was interested, but had a top price point of $7,000. He came over, checked it out, loved it, handed over the money and took it away. It is now in an abandoned coal mine attraction.

The reason I went for eBay in this instance was its shear size and weight – too heavy to sell at a swap meet, too big to be in the antiques mall. It was also so niche I was unlikely to have been able to sell it any other way and in the end, I was relatively lucky.

Some of my friends say there is no better sound than the ding of your laptop, smartphone or tablet when you make a sale on eBay. When I heard that ding with the carousel, it really was music to my ears and my wallet. A $6,500 profit – but one that took plenty of time to happen.

USING THE BLUEPRINT: THE INTERNET

This lesson is purposefully short and sharp, as the internet is a real Pandora's box when it comes to resale, and in fact life in general. You could write an entire book about online buying and selling – all we've done here is scratch the surface, otherwise this lesson could have been very long. Use the internet as the resource it is intended to be and remember it is not the be-all-and-end-all of resale.

- Use the internet as a tool and resource for instant valuing, instant selling, instant buying and instant information.
- Use your time correctly and don't fall into resale rabbit holes and end up losing focus.
- The internet is full of scams and tricks. Make sure you're wise to them.
- Establish your own internet blueprint – it could be sensible to be a hybrid seller.

- Don't just default to eBay – use the internet to find niche auctions and other places to sell online for potentially bigger profits.
- YouTube is an easy place to see if someone has already gone down a similar resale route. Knowledge is power.
- Don't just base sales data on one sale or on asking prices. Make sure you do your homework to establish true value. Use eBay sold prices and Worth Point to gather as much resale data as possible.
- Do due diligence on any website you're using and check reviews.
- Online marketplaces can be a great place to sell unique and niche items you haven't already established a buyer for. Just don't expect instant results.

RESOURCES

WorthPoint (www.worthpoint.com) – an online research site and pricing database for antiques and collectibles.

END OF PART III

Are you inspired? Do you just want to get out there and start flipping items for profit, both your core bread-and-butter stuff and niche goods? Job done!

We bet as you've been reading these pages, you've been able to smell the onions frying at the car boot sale, feel the coats on the clothes rack in the charity shop, visualize an autumnal day in leafy Sussex browsing antiques shops, feel the gravel crunch under your feet at the estate sale, hear the gavel drop at a speciality auction and picture yourself in your pyjamas listing items on the internet.

This book has been a feast for the senses, hasn't it? But this is just the start of your resale journey. Your journey into never going broke.

You can keep stacking up the free cash for your resale pot as we outlined in Part I. You can keep adapting your own resale blueprint we discussed in Part II to all of the great places in Part III to buy and sell.

As you keep going, you'll become more experienced, ever more streamlined. We now anoint you Resale King or Queen (in training).

LESSON 99.9: GO YOUR OWN WAY

This is the last lesson but, for you, it's just the beginning. It's time to fly the book nest and get started on your buying and selling adventure like the soaring, money-making eagle you're about to become.

Like Fleetwood Mac (almost) sang, 'Teaching you, is the right thing to do'. And as Fleetwood Mac did actually sing, 'Go your own way.'

It's time to get out there and buy and sell, using our tips. No two people will follow the same route. Everyone has different interests and goals when buying and selling. Don't get caught up overthinking it. You'll realize that after you've made some money from Part I of this book, Part II and III are where the real fun lies.

As you've hopefully understood while reading this book, it is up to you to decide which resale paths you choose to take. There is no right way to climb that resale mountain. There is no incorrect way to use this book – rather, we hope we've given you inspiration to get started and there is no time like the present.

We want to reiterate that this is only a general framework of what to do and what not to do. It is not a step-by-step set of instructions – hold my hand, sell this exact item, hunt down this exact item, become rich. It is more about utilizing your time, the resources available to everyone, and your nous to make profits – no matter how small.

Remember Lesson 0? There, we set the rules of how to play the resale game. It was a precursor to what was coming. Lesson 99.9 is not really a lesson either. It is a parting shot for you to refresh your memory as you start your journey of buying and selling. It's a post-cursor.

What about Lessons 17–99.8? They are yours to learn as you go. We've given you the groundwork and the ideas, it's time to fill the blanks, have fun and make some money.

GET STARTED. RIGHT NOW

There is no greater risk to your success in the buying and selling game than procrastination. Don't sit around surfing the internet on your smartphone or watching yet another episode of a boxset on television. Wouldn't you rather be making some extra money? What's stopping you? If you need extra motivation to get started right away, these are our tips:

1. Make it part of your day. Try to make £10 rather than watching another episode of your television show. If you are watching television, at least dual-screen and make money while you're doing it.
2. Sell an item in your home and feel the buzz of the sale. Then think about doing it bigger and better – how that will feel?
3. You may realize pretty quickly that you're good at this – the haggling, sniffing out niche items and starting your own little mini resale empire. Honestly, it's good fun.
4. Don't set unrealistic goals: treat it as a way to have fun. When someone asks about your hobby, won't it be great when you say 'Making money from nowhere'?
5. Making money is like going for a run. You know you'll feel better for doing it and you'll be healthier and happier too.
6. If you are lacking the motivation to get into your running gear, put on those trainers and get out in the rain, just remember how you'll feel afterwards. Euphoric!

THE KEY TAKEAWAYS

These are the key takeaways from this book:

- Seize every opportunity to grab free cash to reinvest. That way, any risk is minimal. Keep your pot of free money separate and make sure you're not tempted to fritter it away. This is your foundation.

- Decide what it is you're trying to achieve. Are you aiming to make money after falling on hard times, make money on the side with an already stable income or make money as a hobby?

- Remember not to bite off more than you can chew.

- This book won't make you a millionaire.

- Revisit the parts of the book that are most relevant to you as your resale venture progresses.

- Try reinvesting the profits you have made as you start raising your financial stakes. From pennies to Porsches, see how far you can take it.

HOW HAVE YOU FARED?

How much money have you managed to make following the advice in *Never Go Broke*? Let us know your success stories on social media: @nevergobrokeUK

Or fill in the table below, take a picture and send it to us. We love to hear your stories.

ITEM/PROJECT	MONEY SPENT	MONEY MADE	PROFIT
			TOTAL PROFIT

BUT HOW HAVE WE FARED?

Well, Jesse and Lee will be putting all the tips from Part I into action. From there, we will reinvest the money following our own advice in Parts II and III, to make as much profit as we can – all for charity.

You can follow our journey via our social media: @nevergobrokeUK

INDEX

ACKNOWLEDGEMENTS

We'd like to thank our agent Sarah Williams and the Sophie Hicks Agency, the fantastic team at Octopus, and each other, for making this book happen.

Lee took a deep dive into Jesse's fabulous brain and scooped out the information, taking just the tasty mint choc chip bits.

JM: Svool Yfgglm, dv wrw rg! Ru R dlfow szev glow blf 5 bvzih ztl gszg R dlfow yv dirgrmt gsrh gl blf rm nb yllp, dlfow blf yvorvev nv? Gszmp blf uli yvrmt gsviv uli nv. Gsilfts xzmxvi, gsilfts lfi dliow gizevoh, lfi yfhrmvhhvh, zmw nlhg rnkligzmgob, lfi ufm. R xzm'g dzrg gl hvv dszg rh mvcg uli fh.

R olev blf Mrxlov, zmw R zodzbh droo.

LB: A huge thank you to my wonderful wife Danielle and delightful daughter Brooke. Both make me laugh and smile without fail every day. I'll never be broke with you two in my life.

To my lovely mum Carol, for all the help and unwavering support over the years, my dad Derek, for his encouragement, alongside the rest of my family but especially my sister Lorna, a queen of thrift. Thanks also to Bryan, Lorraine and John.

Additional shout-outs to friends that inspire me all the time, especially Jordan Pillai and Cemil Alkis, along with Chris Kelly, Dan Hyde, Victoria Bischoff and Laura Shannon.

And finally to *This is Money* editor Simon Lambert: thanks a million for all of the help and guidance you've given me in the last decade. It's been invaluable.

LEE BOYCE

Lee Boyce is a financial journalist and assistant editor at *This is Money*, part of the world's largest online newspaper, the *Mail Online*. He studied creative writing and journalism at university, before going on to gain his NCTJ.

In the past decade, he has written serious investigations into mis-selling at Britain's banks to viral pieces about coins and bank notes, read by millions. From investing to pensions, motoring to holidays, there is no topic he hasn't covered when it comes to the pound in your pocket.

He is co-star of the *This is Money* podcast, writes the popular weekly *Consumer Trends* column and has had stories published in the *Daily Mail*.

Despite his daughter Brooke only being two years-old, Lee tries to hammer home the importance of compound interest and quantitative easing during playtime. He believes you're never too young, or old, to learn about personal finance and its importance.

He lives in Rayleigh, Essex with his wonderful wife Danielle and when he is not all consumed by writing about money, he loves long walks in his beautiful native county, far flung exotic jaunts or simply sitting in his favourite chair with rescue cat Cali on his lap, ice-cold beer in hand.

 @lee_boyce

JESSE McCLURE

Jesse McClure, often known as the Resale King, has been on television worldwide over the last decade buying up treasures to earn some sweet cash.

From his humble beginnings growing up in his family antique mall in Los Angeles, he has taken his encyclopedic knowledge of antiques and collectibles and spun it into global TV hits, including *Storage Hunters*, *Storage Hunters UK* and *British Treasure, American Gold*.

But as a jack-of-all-trades, he hasn't limited himself to just a glorified junk salesman. From breaking Guinness world records to travelling the world, Jesse seeks not only to buy and sell it all, but also to experience it all as well, getting there via Lilly, his trusted 1978 Pontiac Trans Am.

When he isn't working, he enjoys cheap pizza, expensive whiskey and long naps. His favourite thing to do though is snuggle his petite but fiery Essex wife Nicole.

 @jessemcclure
 theresaleking
 resaleking

NEVERGOBROKE.CO.UK

Britain is blessed with a wealth of fantastic financial publications, with money sections of newspapers taken far more seriously since the credit crunch and the quality of journalism available now unbelievably strong.

But many miss out on reading important money content, perhaps labelling financial news and guides as 'boring' or 'not their thing'. Meanwhile, we'd have a serious chunk of cash if given a pound for every time someone tells us, 'I wish there was more financial education at school'.

What we say is this: The internet is your friend. Answers to all of your money questions can be found quickly and easily now, with a raft of excellent and trustworthy sources online.

With *Never Go Broke*, both this book and our social media and website, we're not focusing on ways to build huge piles of wealth. (That can be done with pensions and investments, saving frugally and making good money–life decisions, and by arming yourself with the knowledge easily available at your fingertips.) *Never Go Broke* aims to help put some money in your pocket <u>TODAY</u> with simple wins that the majority of people can do easily in a language you can understand and with action that can be taken straight away. No huge investment pot needed. No degree needed. No interest in the intricacies of the money markets needed.

What you do with the money you make is your prerogative, but we believe that taking cash made today and investing it into <u>TOMORROW</u> with simple resale tips is a great way to make a crust, and keep your cash working in an upward spiral, while even having a bit of fun as you do.

Money makes the world go round. Most people spend their entire lives trying to get more of it. *Never Go Broke* can help you do just that.